Lis Dorer

D1335083

SWANS IN MY KITCHEN

The Story of a Swan Sanctuary

Lis Dorer

The Book Castle

This revised edition published March 1995
First published October 1992
by
The Book Castle
12 Church Street
Dunstable
Bedfordshire LU5 4RU

© Lis Dorer, 1992, 1995

The right of Lis Dorer to be identified as the Author of this Work has been asserted by her in accordance with the Copyright, Designs and Patents Act 1988.

ISBN 1 871199 62 X

Front cover: A swan in my kitchen ungergoing treatment.   A.G.

Back cover: My husband carrying Princess along the
Grand Union canal to a joyful reunion with
Houdini who is waiting for her. M.Y.

Computer typeset by Keyword, Aldbury, Hertfordshire.
Printed by Alden Press, Oxford.

All rights reserved.

INTRODUCTION

Awarded the Silver Cross of St. George by 'This England', for her work with injured swans, Lis Dorer has written 'Swans in my Kitchen' to tell how she became interested in swan rescue. She eventually set up a sanctuary, comprising garden, river and lake, to look after the casualties along our waterways until they become well enough to be released back into the wild.

Over the years 'The Swan Lady' has told of her experiences on radio and television, including 'Animal Country' with Desmond Morris and Sarah Kennedy, and featured in numerous Press articles as well as in 'Bella' and 'Wild About Animals', all drawing the attention of the public to the plight of the swan.

Today many places, especially in Hertfordshire, Bedfordshire and Buckinghamshire, have thriving swan families due to Lis constantly rescuing and admitting them for treatment, or helping them out of difficulties and returning them to their natural environment. She also co-operates extensively with many ornithological experts and organisations, so that her unique experience and knowledge can help further research into the swan's lifestyle and predicament.

Her work has meant giving 24 hours a day all the year round to be on call to attend to rescues and running the sanctuary, but the hours devoted to the birds she considers well spent when a paralysed swan staggers to its feet again, and takes its first steps back to life.

'Swans in my Kitchen' is the heart-warming story of one woman's dedication to fight for the survival of these beautiful birds. Its many tales and anecdotes are full of the sense of humour and love with which she confronts the inevitable tragic moments.

All royalties from the book will go to the work of 'Swan Care', the entirely voluntary service she operates from her sanctuary at 'Bourneside', 14 Moorland Road, Boxmoor, Hemel Hempstead, Hertfordshire, HP1 1NH. Tel (0442) 251961.

AUTHOR'S ACKNOWLEDGEMENTS

I have written this book in response to popular demand, as a small record of happenings whilst rescuing various birds, especially swans.

At the same time I am hoping it will raise some funds for the work to continue, and it is dedicated to the many friends I have made over the years, whose interest and vigilance enables me to reach sickly birds before it is too late.

Special dedication is made to Chris Sander of Johnson, Daniels & Partners, Cassiobury Drive, Watford, Herts., Veterinary Surgeons, without whose interest, help and support it would not have been possible to save our swans.

Most of all, my thanks go to my husband, Terry, for his patience and understanding of what drives me on to fight for the swans against all the odds. Without his support in every way, life would have been even more difficult. He puts up with being dragged out to mend sheds, fix runs, fetch shavings from the woodyard, helps with treatments, not to mention the occasional rescue with which I need help, traipsing miles lumbered with rescue equipment, swan hooks, etc. when he does have his own work to do as well, otherwise we will all sink without trace!

Finally, my kind friends at Dacorum Business Machines at Warners End, Hemel Hempstead, especially Bill Goss, who have come to 'my rescue' so many times.

Swan Care

Lis Dorer has dedicated her life to the rescue of Swans in our Area.

Her base is in Boxmoor Hemel Hempstead were she works out of her Home.

Lis's work is voluntary and we try to help by raising funds for her at Fairs and Charity events.

We are currently collecting Bric A Brac and any unwanted Christmas presents.

If you have any items you wish to donate please drop them off at :-

19 Sherfield Avenue

Rickmansworth

Or if you would like us to collect them please call

01923 773700 (evenings)

Her book "Swans in My Kitchen" is available from the above address price £2.99

Alternatively we would welcome cheque donations which should be made payable to Swan Care & sent direct to:-

Lis Dorer

14 Moorland Road

Boxmoor, Hemel Hempstead

Herts HP1 1NH

FOREWORD
by
Dr Philip Burton, Vice-Chairman, Hawk and Owl Trust and formerly Principal Scientific Officer, British Museum (Natural History), Tring

This book gives a fascinating insight into the lifestyle of a remarkable lady. Her garden by the trout fishery lake is one I visit at intervals, usually to ring some of its avian inhabitants. However I have never before heard the full story of Swan Care, from its simple beginnings to the skilled and efficient service it now provides. My own commitments nowadays are mainly to birds of prey, but wildfowl (Brent Geese in particular) were my first love, and I can relate to many of the events that Lis describes in this book. Sometimes these are sad ones, involving damage done to birds and their environment by the ignorance or indifference of man. Others are funny or even bizarre; one inevitable consequence of a life that revolves around wild creatures is that one must expect the unexpected. Lis's experiences range from the offer of brandy from a nun materialising out of the gloaming as she lifts a swan over a five-barred gate to the excitement of a swimming pool attendant wishing to see a swan's teeth! Above all, though, this is the story of the love of a beautiful bird and dedication to its care in a hostile world. Giving all credit where it is due to responsible anglers and others, Lis Dorer nevertheless makes painfully clear the needless suffering and damage which still results from human carelessness or cruelty. Long may her devotion, and that of others like her, continue to redress the balance and foster more enlightened attitudes.

SWAN CARE

An entirely voluntary service
operated by Lis Dorer to
rescue swans in distress.

All donations gratefully received.

'Bourneside'. 14 Moorland Road, Boxmoor,
Hemel Hempstead, Hertfordshire, HP1 1NH
Tel: 0442 251961

CONTENTS

Photographic Acknowledgements

A.G.   Andrew Garner

B.G.   Bob Gannon, Insight. Courtesy of Bella Magazine

P.W.   Peter Ward, Hemel Hempstead Gazette & Express Newspapers

J.C.   John Child, Hemel Hempstead Gazette & Express Newspapers

H.K.   Hank Kemme. Courtesy of Wild About Animals

D.S.   David Satchell, Review Group Newspapers

M.Y.   Mick Young, Review Group Newspapers

R.N.   Review Group Newspapers

S.C.   Swan Care

Part 1

The Swan Sanctuary

A view of the sanctuary taken from the river.　　　　　A.G.

Chapter 1

WHERE ?

I live in paradise.

My garden slopes down to a river, over which a small bridge leads to a trout lake – a haven for wildlife. Beyond is the Grand Union canal, with its boats passing up and down while people walk their dogs along the towpath. Another small river runs alongside, before an expanse of moorland which is used during the summer months for grazing sheep and cows. The busy A41 borders the other side of the moor, adjacent to Hemel Hempstead railway station, so we can see cars and trains as well. At the back of the station the land rises to woodland towards the hamlet of Felden, where a balloonist lives, so we even watch balloons rising over the horizon on nice days. There is always something to enjoy in the varied scene from my lounge window.

Apart from watching the birds undergoing treatment in my garden sanctuary, it is interesting to see others come to take up residence in the various bird boxes around the garden and lake, or build nests along the hedgerows and in the trees. The kingfisher calls along the riverbank, but we never know who the next arrival will be, so our binoculars are kept at the ready. The lake plays host to various ducks rescued and/or hatched by foster-mother birds in the sanctuary, and we have a resident pair of swans living on the lake. Every now and then a passing swan may try to drop in with a view to staking a claim, but he is soon sent packing by the irate resident cob, intent on protecting his territory, although he does tolerate other small waterbirds and Canada Geese. Currently this pair of swans are known as P19 and Lady; P19 arrived some years ago from another area, and only came to my attention when he got tied up in fishing line on the canal. I disentangled him, and he stayed, attracted to a female on the same stretch of water, and since our lake was 'vacant' at the time, moved in with his 'Lady'. One visitor we would rather be without is the fox, who calls regularly around the lake and garden, supplementing his diet with a tasty morsel of birdlife if the opportunity presents itself. In 1987 he gobbled up four cygnets hatched twenty-four hours previously by P19 and Lady, and everyone was sad.

Our 'resident' swans, P19 and Lady with their 1988 brood on the river at the bottom of the garden. A.G.

Occasionally a heron descends for a visit, and for a while we had a regular pair whom I called Henry and Henrietta, but our water is not as shallow as they like for wading, so although it was possible to have a passing stab at the fish, after a while they moved on elsewhere, where presumably the 'pickings' are better. Canada geese arrive frequently, making a great commotion, especially now they have increased in numbers and become a native bird. They move up and down the valley, visiting all the places where they know they will find food.

Nowadays I have eleven sheds around the garden to contain the various birds at night and keep them safe against the fox. In the early days I had only a small pond in the garden, and it took quite a long time before I could afford a swan-size pool, plus a concrete surround with brick edging and gravel.

We still have a certain amount of grass in our back garden, but gone are the flowers and vegetables. The garden has been pecked clean of what most people cherish, but at least we do not have to worry about cutting the lawn. From time to time I still persevere with putting in a few bedding plants, but the geese think they are delicious – they eat the tops with vigour, then sit down on what is left, before finally pulling up the roots and munching them with great enjoyment. Great is the excitement these days if I do start to potter about in the garden, since in no time flat I am surrounded by interested chickens, ducks and geese, all anxious to help.

Luckily, we have quite a few trees and hedging plants, bordering the garden, some of which flower at various times, plus an apple and cherry tree and several hazel nut bushes which attract squirrels. There are also apple trees across the other side of the lake, and willows growing along the side of the canal. In Winter the view is far-reaching through bare branches, but as Spring arrives and all the leaves break through, we are surrounded by greenery in all directions.

When Autumn comes the birds have a great time bobbing for apples in the lake to supplement their diet, and others enjoy nibbling windfalls on the grass. Personally, I do not like the Autumn, although I can appreciate the beautiful colours, but the prospect of the onset of Winter makes life difficult when dishes freeze to the ground, and the pond and hose are frozen. Sheds need clearing out even more frequently as rain and snow blow inside, and it also means hazardous journeys to birds in trouble.

I am always pleased when Christmas is over, as life is so hectic anyway that I do not have time to indulge in a relaxing Christmas as well. For me Christmas is like every other day if I can save the life of a bird needing help, and let it go again fit and well, and it is also a time when calls continue to arrive. My family never know if I will be around to shop and prepare for the festivities, and despite good intentions, I always seem to end up sitting in the vets' surgery on Christmas Eve clutching a variety of birds needing attention before the holiday. Since there are so few people who rescue wildlife, especially at

Christmas time, it is nothing to find myself rushing off to a third rescue by eleven o'clock in the morning, which my family get cross about, but it is an unusual luxury travelling down a deserted M25 to Waltham Abbey perhaps, hoping to untie a swan festooned with fishing line. Later I particularly love the excitement as Spring approaches and you can feel the sap rising, and the prospect of glorious sunny days makes it easier to cast care aside. A time when more people venture afield, and exchange a smile and a few words of greeting as they cross the moor, or walk along the towpath.

This is the kind of rubbish with which swans get entangled. A.G.

So this is where, for me, it all happens – some little excitement amongst the birds in the garden, river and lake is always afoot – life never stands still, and a day spent away from here seems like a month, making the prospect of a holiday, even if we had been able to afford one over the last decade, something to be viewed with trepidation. A place where friends love to visit and linger while envying the green tranquillity of our outlook, and the fun of watching the happiness of the birds who inhabit this beautiful place.

Living in the sanctuary there is also a selection of chickens who, apart from supplying genuine free range eggs, additionally provide the best hatching medium for any eggs after the death of a mother bird. It started with a farmer friend giving me a black bantam named Mrs Black, who hatched out Solo, a gosling, with whom she raised several ducks and a cygnet. A chicken is much better than an incubator in a sanctuary, since the chicks receive aftercare, are soon marched into the shed if it starts to rain, and are protected from the attentions of other animals or birds. However, when the babies grow and become more independent, the chicken is rather confused when offspring with webbed feet take to the water.

If I have to take in a number of ducklings and have no suitable foster mother, and they are very tiny, I put them in a cardboard box on a heated pad with an old-fashioned string mophead strung across the top of the box so the babies can huddle beneath it, and they think they are tucked under their mother. I feed them on a diet of chick crumbs and water, and they usually thrive by this means.

Sometimes I am asked to take other adult birds to live here, as was the case with a number of ducks and geese living with someone who had helped out the Aylesbury Wildlife Hospital now and again, but who had become too poorly to cope with them any longer. Les and Sue Stocker who run that service used to be very limited for space in the original hospital run at their home, although now they have splendid new facilities.

Winter 1987/1988 was very wet and when this new contingent arrived they were a little bewildered after their journey, but soon dried and cleaned themselves in a shed with plenty of straw. Next day they emerged into a straw yard in which to forage, a run with grass to eat, and best of all, a pond in which to bathe. The noise they made when they stumbled into the water was deafening, and I wish I had recorded their cries of excitement as they dipped and dived in and out of the water, then rose and flapped their wings. Their excitement attracted the attention of the birds already living in the wild over the lake, and they all started calling to one to the other, particularly the new Canada geese and the resident pair on the lake, Ebb and Flow. After a few weeks I let them out into the rest of the garden, the river and the lake, and they were so pleased to have new territory to explore.

At the same time, I also acquired a pair of Indian Runners. This is a breed of duck, without shoulders, who hold themselves very erect on land, and really are most amusing to watch. I called them Salt and Pepper since this best described their colouring. I have heard Indian Runners described as hock bottles on legs – they hold their wings crossed at the tips behind their backs, and seem to be on tippy toes when running. Definitely guaranteed to bring a smile to most faces. Since then I have taken in a white Indian Runner with an injured leg whom I named Pinta, followed by three blacks who are known as the Inky Boys.

Every year sees a steady flow of swans large and small in and out of the sanctuary. Calls for help to swans dying as a result of swallowing fishing tackle continue well into the close season, which means the chance of successful treatment is very low. Last year we were still treating some cases when the coarse fishing season opened again in June. Early in May the first cygnet was trapped behind an old metal railing embedded in the canal bank immediately below the swan's nest in Berkhamsted; I had already rescued the parents in previous years. Mum was still sitting on the nest, and Dad was standing guard over the trapped baby nearly three days old. I crept between them, and managed to manoeuvre the little one out, and found he had a damaged wing and leg, and was very cold, having endured two sharp frosts out of the nest squeaking for help. I brought him home for intensive care, and named him Georgie. So Georgie got over his bad start to life, and became quite a character. Once or twice he accompanied me when I gave talks about Swan Care, and received quite a welcome from the children at Cassiobury Infants School, Watford, who went on to raise some money to help bring him up.

After Georgie I had a procession of other cygnets who had either been abandoned for some reason or got injured. I had two greasy twins who had been abandoned at Croxley Green, followed shortly afterwards by another cygnet from the same area floating up and down on the River Gade. These three I named Richard, James and Edward. Then came Henry from Bedford who had insisted on trotting up and down someone's garden and wanting to stay despite being put back in the water, but obviously he was too small to survive on land on his own. He was followed by a cygnet from the canal at Apsley near Hemel Hempstead, who developed chronic bronchitis, which was very worrying since he was acting as foster mother to a day-old duckling, who arrived at the same time and was very comforted by being able to snuggle up to William, as this cygnet was christened.

William and his Ducky friend were confined to a bedroom with plenty of ventilation, where I lit a Wright's Vaporizer to help William's rough breathing, and gave him daily injections, and the little duck tucked up close. We were delighted when, after a few days, the noisy breathing eased and William was obviously so much better, and in due course both birds progressed down the garden into the sanctuary proper where they remained good friends, sitting side by side together every night in their shed. Eventually William was released into the wild, but the duck still pops in and out from the lake to see if William has returned.

Next they were joined by John Boy ex Letchworth, rescued by Alan Janes, an RSPCA Inspector. John Boy had a broken toe, which became swollen and was x-rayed at Johnson, Daniels & Partners; treatment was put in hand and he soon recovered.

Soon all cygnets become totally 'swan' and do much socialising in and out of the water with any adult patients who may be passing through, and these youngsters soon became attached to a young bird from the previous year with a fractured ankle and lead poisoning, and a pen who had to be taken away from her cygnets because her leg was sliced open by a fishing hook, and her wing reduced to raw meat by fishing line, none of which was noticed until infection was well advanced. Her youngsters were brought up by her mate. She had to undergo two operations before the leg was successfully healed, but after that she made great strides towards complete recovery.

Meantime, another outbreak of botulism resulted in a batch

of dead cygnets, one of whom I managed to save, and Little Joe soon made up for lost time and was eventually released at Tring Reservoirs with two other cygnets who came along for care later.

So as well as first aid in my kitchen this is the sanctuary the birds find when they need help.

Chapter 2

WHY ?

The question I am most often asked is how I come to be doing swan rescue. Basically, the answer is that having moved to a house with a garden adjacent to a river, on the other side of which is trout lake which is host to passing birds, my interest was triggered off when a pair of swans came along one Spring with five cygnets, having been 'bottled off' their nest in Hemel Hempstead Water Gardens. I spotted them down in the river, took away the wire along the bottom of the garden so they could come on the lawn, and so began my love affair with the mute swan.

I remember noting at the time the utter disbelief and amazement of our hitherto country cats when suddenly confronted by the biggest birds they had ever seen – you could see them thinking, 'Well, I've seen some big birds in my time, but nothing as large as this!' In fact, my black male cat, Thomas, did not continue to give them the respect they deserve, and one day I saw he had a large bare, red patch on his back where obviously he had been pecked by a swan; subsequently, it turned septic and he needed treatment, but it has meant that Thomas gives all swans a wide berth.

That Summer was the first of many when our garden has been occupied by swans in various stages of growth. It was a marvellous sight to see the family of swans come up the garden 'Sunday School style', Mum in front, youngsters behind in single file, being followed at the rear by proud Dad. They came regularly through the conservatory door and over the doorstep into the kitchen; if I ignored their arrival they would tap the breadbin to remind me why they had come to call. It was not unusual to hear the patter of webbed feet across the kitchen floor on their way into the lounge. Our visitors were liable to leap from their chairs as swans flapped their wings and walked right up to the hearth. At that time access to the stairs was from the lounge, and I remember coming indoors one day and finding half-a-dozen geese standing on the lower landing gazing up the flight of stairs and chattering amongst themselves as if to decide who would be the first to go up! I had to be very gentle in persuading them to return to the garden via the lounge doors before they left any nasty deposits.

So many Summer days in those early years were spent on the lawn, surrounded by swans, geese, ducks, cats and dogs, not to mention the occasional rabbit or two – sheer peace and harmony. However, it was not until our pair of swans had seen off their youngsters, and Mr Swan returned alone, that I ceased to take them for granted. We were distressed that obviously something had happened to Mrs Swan, but we never knew what. Mr Swan was very sad and lonely, and he stayed with us all the Winter. He lived on the lake, and spent much time toiling up the garden to sit about, and seemed to find some small consolation in our friendship. He would sit under our bedroom window in the morning and 'call' me, then my husband would say, 'You must be the only woman in Hertfordshire being courted by a swan, you'd better go and see him!' So down I would go and give him a few kind words, and promise that one day a lovely young swan would come along for him.

One day this lovely young swan did materialise out of the canal, and my husband opened the gate of the lake in order that she could come in. Mr Swan soon made friends and brought her up the garden to show me. For a little while we thought everything was going well but shortly after a female bird came swimming down the river and Mr Swan went to chat her up too, and in the final event he took up with the newcomer, and ditched his previous girlfriend. It was a pity because his newer mate was very young, and only just old enough to breed. In due course a nest was built beyond the lake, and eggs laid, but only one hatched. The parents continued to sit, obviously hoping for more babies, and meanwhile, the only cygnet kept going walkies on his own and getting into all sorts of trouble, including actually crossing the road one day. He had to be brought home by my son and thereafter insisted on following him about; however, we persevered with replacing him in the nest, but were very sorry one day when a neighbour telephoned to say her cat had just brought home a cygnet, and it had died.

After this the parents left the lake, but returned after a little while looking a bit tatty. I thought they had probably been in a dispute, until, having taken my car into the garage one day, I was walking home along the canal when I spotted Mr Swan loitering under some overhanging branches on the opposite side of the water. I called him, and he came slowly over, looking really sick, the bottom of his neck resting on his back, and his whole demeanour that of a bird in trouble. At the same time I found Mr Swan's wife sitting on the bank further along the canal, and she too was very sick. I rushed home and

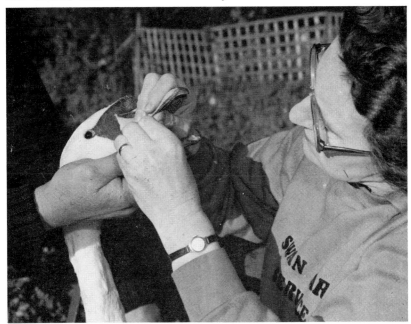

This swan had a fish hook in his tongue.   *A.G.*

13

eventually found out about Swan Rescue in Norfolk, and Len Baker came to help us.

On this occasion we laid poor Mr Swan on the bank, and in due course found he had a fishing hook embedded in his tongue which had turned green, with several others down his throat, together with 30ft of fishing line – his webbed feet were torn, and needless to say he was badly poisoned. His mate was also poisoned.

This incident finally made me aware that swans do not just glide about on water looking beautiful, and I started to look closely at swans for signs of lead poisoning in particular. I also started searching for books and information about swans, though this was easier said than done. I did find out that by 1978 the flock of swans at Stratford-upon-Avon had disappeared, and the numbers of other swans along the Thames had dropped dramatically. Various scientific bodies, including the Edward Grey Institute of Field Ornithology, came up with results of investigation into the cause, and it was found on carrying out post mortem examination that lead weights discarded by fishermen were the most common cause for death. Having found that the mature birds in my own area had succumbed to lead, I realised that the young ones would have to survive until four years old before they would be able to breed, and I determined to set about putting more effort into their care; and so began my real work.

Chapter 3

WHAT ?

The mute swan, or to give it the name which does justice to this majestic bird, 'Cygnus Olor' is our largest native swan, and is certainly not mute. The mixtures of snorts and hisses vary widely, but can be frightening and a sign of impending danger to onlookers, particularly in the breeding season.

He is found on fairly large areas of still water, such as slow-flowing rivers, lakes and gravel pits, and in this area, the canal. Briefly, he is big, white and beautiful. He has a small head with a grey/orange beak (depending on age) pointing downwards, a black, fleshy knob over the nostrils, which is usually larger in the mature male bird, and a very long, graceful neck leading into a big, armful of body, in all measuring from bill to tail about 4–5 ft. The long neck enables him to bottom feed on underwater plants and pondweed, and pick up the grit he needs.

Swans pair off at around 3–4 years, the cob, or male, selecting a nest site near the water where nesting material is available, and in due course the pen, or female, carries out much of the work involved, constantly adding to the nest around her as she sits. If satisfactory, the same site is used year after year, and it is interesting to note that even successive pairs of swans choose to nest at the same site although they have not previously seen that place used for nesting.

The pen lays an egg every other day for up to 12 days from

April to June, and does most of the incubating – the cob taking his turn now and again; otherwise he is engaged in guarding the area around the nest, particularly disliking anything that is white. After 35 days or so the eggs hatch, and the cygnets emerge with their eyes open, covered in soft, grey down. In a couple of days they leave the nest, returning at night, and then venture further on to the water away from the nest area. They learn to fly at around four months, and are driven away by Dad at the latest by early Spring, by which time their plumage is changing from grey to nearly white. They fly at an average speed of 35 miles per hour. When young they gather in flocks, but as they mature, seek a partner, though they do not always mate for life. I have observed several changes of partner. However, normally they settle down happily with a mate, and stay together until something happens to either one or the other. Having lost a partner, they usually seek another.

Our lake is operated as a trout fishery, and during the fishing season we have various fishermen trying to catch their quota of trout. No way could I ever cast a line to catch a

Boxmoor Trout Fishery – an aerial view of the lake – the garden sanctuary is amongst the trees on the right of the photograph. S.C.

beautiful trout, and then kill the poor thing by bashing it over the head with, of all the inaptly named equipment, 'a priest'. However, responsible, well-run fishing syndicates do not cause anything like the damage to wildlife that is so prevalent on open waterways like canals, where there are not enough bailiffs to check on the use of lead, or possession of the necessary licence.

Since fishermen generally have been accused of doing so much harm to wildlife, most of them are very anxious to be seen to care, and it is very sad that some indiscriminate fishermen littering the waterways with their lethal rubbish give everyone else a bad name. I have actually received donations from fishing clubs, and I really appreciate their help – instead of being met with abuse, my efforts to help the swans have received friendly consideration and help. Many fishermen do care about wildlife and the environment, and do much to keep bad water clean and flowing, and it is only the bad experiences I have of those who flagrantly harm swans, which result in my being called out, which make me angry; if only they could see the suffering they occasion birds and be more careful, my workload would be eased and the birds left to pass their lives peacefully in what little territory remains. It is a fact that when

'Ben' the moorhen who arrived tied up with fishing line which had cut off the blood supply to one leg which eventually fell off, but he survived. P.W.

17

the coarse fishing season closes in March, gradually the number of calls to rescue birds tied up with fishing tackle decreases, and likewise within hours of the coarse fishing season commencing again in June, the telephone calls start to come in straight away.

When I am called out I never know what obstacles await me – wire fences, weirs, steep banks, bridges, locks, to name a few, and more often than not the need to wade about in water; sometimes the frustration of another bird coming between me and the object of my rescue, causing an unexpected plunge into the water. Needless to say I try to keep a spare pair of dry wellingtons handy, and am not too upset at crawling out soaking wet. I am sometimes asked why I am not frightened of swans, and when confronted by an irate cob intent on avoiding capture I do feel a twinge of trepidation, but a sick bird needs help, and fear is driven away by concern. Obviously a very sick swan which cannot stand presents no trouble, and only requires firm and gentle handing to reassure and calm. Often the degree of damage and sickness is apparent by his inability to move away and fight back, though he may fight to free his wings when picked up and thrash his feet about, and some have a habit of biting. A badly leaded swan is like picking up an empty cushion as compared to a weighty bird in the earliest stages of debilitation.

Chapter 4

HOW ?

Animals of various kinds have always played an important part in my life. As a little girl I used to help an old lady look after the chickens in her orchard, and I grew up in close proximity to pigs, cows and horses. We had cats, dogs and rabbits at home, and during my early married life we kept pigs, chickens and rabbits on a smallholding. I became accustomed to being presented with baby pigs to bottle feed and look after indoors, and at that time our milkman used to say, 'I never know what is going to come out over your doorstep, a pig, a dog or a baby!' Neighbours were very amused to see a little pink pig or two accompany me to the washing line whist hanging out nappies, then trot back behind my heels indoors again.

However, I digress, that is another story. Nowadays we live elsewhere, close to a main road, easy for people to reach and surrounded by water for birds to reach. When we have a hard Winter, many birds fly in from surrounding areas, since even if the canal and lake freeze over, the river Bulbourne keeps moving, and somehow or other I supply the food. People bring me bread from time to time, and I used to visit an old people's home to collect bits and pieces. Fortunately, at the present time I am able to collect some bread from a local supermarket, and another delivers left-over bread when it is available, and this is a great help. Generally it is important that swans mainly eat mixed corn and wheat, together with vegetables, weed and grit.

In the early days of my rescue activities, I endeavoured to run a same-day typing service, but typing late into the night to meet deadlines become too much after chasing sick birds during the day, so I decided it was more important to restore swans to this part of the country, and try to combat the misery inflicted upon them by man.

Money has never been plentiful, so when my meagre savings ran out I took to selling anything not really needed. Unfortunately, I had never been interested in jewellery, so I had nothing to fall back on there, but away went any ornaments worth selling, followed by furniture, and finally any of my clothes not used every day went to our local Nearly New Shop. Holidays and socialising had become a thing of the past, so posh clothes were not required anyway. Housekeeping became increasingly difficult, as I tried to feed the family without them realising how close to the wind I was sailing.

However, inevitably the time came when I no longer had anything left worth selling – no more economies could be made, so to help me over the next immediate financial hurdle, I sold my wedding ring. But how helpless I felt when I received three phone calls the next day asking me to rescue a swan at Ware, and had to explain I could not do so because I did not have enough money to put petrol in the car to get there. Thinking back, I wonder why none of the callers cared enough to offer to help. Perhaps they thought like so many others that I get paid for doing this work. I suggested they might find someone else to come

My daughter, Jocelyne, who cycled from London to Brighton a few years ago in aid of Save our Swans at Windsor. P.W.

out, and explained that there was no guarantee the swan could be caught, or even located, straight away, and it might be necessary to return the next day to search again.

Shortly after this I was delighted to hear from the RSPCA that a vet at Rickmansworth might be able to help the swans, and they directed me to Save our Swans at Windsor, run by a veterinary surgeon, Stephen Cooke and his wife, Zyllah. They were working to rescue and treat sick swans in and around Windsor and Maidenhead in particular, but also covered a wide area wherever help was needed, and despite enormous pressure on their time and resources, put in many years' stalwart work to bring the desperate plight of swans to the attention of other people at a time when there were so few swans left on the Thames. They were instrumental in urging the MP for Richmond, Jeremy Hanley, to put a Motion before the House of Commons in 1984 regarding the plight of the swan, and this eventually became law in January 1987, banning the use of all but the smallest lead weights by fishermen, and they were backed up by David Bird of the National Federation of Anglers.

For some time Save our Swans helped me to save many birds around Hemel Hempstead – they did the veterinary work which I did not understand, then I brought the birds back to Boxmoor for rest and recuperation before release back to their territory. Then after seven years of limping from one rescue to another, Save our Swans ran into difficulties themselves, and were no longer able to help me out.

The crunch came on Bank Holiday Saturday when I had been called out to two swans locally from the river and canal, both presenting lead poisoning symptoms. Finally, Roger Johnson of Johnson, Daniels & Partners agreed to help, and suggested I should get in touch with his Partner, Chris Sander, who is interested in birds, and from that time his help has been indispensable. When he is not available, Jim Mason is a great help, and since Johnson, Daniels & Partners is a large Practice, they have a big selection of drugs to hand. Richard Clarke, a vet at Berkhamsted, also helps me out from time to time.

One December evening after this I was called out to Mill End at Rickmansworth where a lady had confined a sick swan from the river at the side of her garden in a shed, so I was able to bring him in for treatment, although it was dark by the time I located her. Tests revealed that this cygnet, whom I called 'Luke', was poisoned and paralysed, and treatment was set in hand. Although he seemed to improve, progress was not maintained, but I did receive a lot of help from the Phoenix Holistic Clinix in Hemel Hempstead who loaned me a Magnetopulse machine, and prescribed various homeopathic drugs. It was interesting to learn of the wonderful work they are doing to help horses in particular, but also the radionic analysis work on hair, and in the swans' case, feathers, whereby a clue is given to the cause of illness.

Luke – a poisoned swan with an injured leg receiving Magnetopulse treatment, a machine which works on magnetic field energy. D.S.

Chapter 5

RESCUE

Swans land in gardens and on roads, all over the place, and seem to be drawn to places like the A41 locally when it is raining, confusing it with the Grand Union Canal which runs parallel. Most times I am able to attend traffic incidents straight away, but even so one October evening when the Hertfordshire Police asked me to go to a swan sitting in the main road between St. Albans and Hemel Hempstead I was still too late. I located the bird straight away, a large cygnet sitting across the white lines in the middle of the road. I parked the car, and made a vain effort to stop the traffic whizzing by – then tragedy struck in the form of a car which drove straight into the bird with a sickening thud – feathers flew everywhere – then someone stopped and I hurried across the road in the falling dusk to gather the shattered swan up in my arms, and ran back to the verge. As I did so, his body fell apart, ripped to pieces. I knelt in the grass cradling him in my arms; his head was cut all over, but he was still alive, his liquid black eyes looking at me; I prayed that he might die quickly, and he did. Sometimes, the swans are already dead at the side of the road by the time I arrive.

A major hazard to swans are electricity cables, and death is usually the outcome of these encounters. In our area the Electricity Board are prepared to fit big plastic spirals along the most dangerous lines, and in other places you may see large, orange plastic balls suspended from power lines, although they tell me these ice up in hard winter weather, thereby interfering with the supply.

Sometimes, for various reasons, swans get out of the water and go 'walkies', which tends to frighten local inhabitants, and passersby, but in most cases it is only necessary to hold out your arms and direct the bird back whence it came, unless the wanderer is bent on escaping from another swan who is angry and trying to protect his territory from the intruder.

One Summer a local cygnet chose to land in a cherry tree in a front garden, which no doubt came as a shock to both bird and householder. I wondered what I was going to find when I was called out, but by the time I arrived the bird had fallen to the ground, and just needed taking into care until he had recovered, and then releasing on to water. Not long afterwards this same bird decided to alight on the open air swimming pool at the local sports centre, where he caused great consternation. I was asked to come and take him away, and I wish all rescues were so easy, since there were several assistants to encourage him towards the steps, from where I

A call to the local swimming pool to rescue this uninvited visitor.   J.C.

was able to pick him up. One of the staff rushed up excitedly to see the swan's teeth, and I explained he had none, only ridges for pulling up weed, etc.

Around the same time I was called to a local oil depot where a swan had landed in an oil pond within a compound. The company had been trying to find someone to help them for ages and were very relieved when I arrived ten minutes later. A man appeared and let me into the compound. He himself waited outside the gate whilst I stalked and eventually managed to pick the bird up, although my coat was covered in oil in the process. Nowadays I have certain clothes for some situations, especially rescuing swans from sewage tanks.

My first rescues were incidental to walking miles up and down waterways checking on swans, but as time went by I became more widely known for my interest in their welfare, and if anyone found a swan in difficulty they would let me know. Gradually other animal rescue organisations, like the RSPCA, found I was very useful to rescue and admit water birds, not to mention the RSPB who themselves do not rescue but are glad to pass on requests for help to someone who does. So now I am on call to several local authorities, and, as already mentioned, the Police, and when the telephone rings I never know who might need advice and/or help.

Since we live in surroundings ideal for locating bird boxes and ringing birds, we got to know several people from The British Trust for Ornithology; a research organisation who are able to provide information for people carrying out surveys, thereby co-ordinating bird observation and conservation, especially helpful to people working on their own throughout the country. Through them, many of the swans I have treated are identified by a numbered metal ring fixed around the lower leg, which if found on a dead bird of any sort should be notified to the British Museum in London. They then advise The British Trust for Ornithology when and where the bird has been found, who relay the information to the ringer. I have also used a large, plastic ring bought from The Wildfowl and Wetlands Trust at Slimbridge which facilitates swan identification from a distance. Quite a number of swans are now marked in this way, increasing interest amongst walkers and those studying bird movements, and more reliable reports of bird activities are the norm. It is no good making assertions about the lives and deaths of swans if no definite proof of identity is available.

My husband, Terry, and I fixing a Darvic ring on a cygnet's leg prior to release.
                                                          B.G.

When called out to a bird in difficulty I arrive to find the swan being given a wide berth by all and sundry, and most are reluctant to assist in cornering the victim if he is up and running again. So a little reassurance is required, and very soon I have gathered the swan up in my arms, making sure his wings are secure. Then he is wrapped carefully in a swan jacket, and popped into a large supermarket-type shopping bag so he can be placed safely in the back of the car to be taken to wherever he has to go. There are occasions, of course, when it is only necessary to put the swan back on his territory, or adjacent water.

I never know what to expect having been called out, and some years ago when a swan was spotted tied up on the river Gade with fishing paraphernalia, I plunged in to grab him and found I was sinking fast into the silt at the bottom of the water, and this is one of the main dangers. Now when I am in new territory I turn my swan hook, which is like a shepherd's crook, up the wrong way, and push the handle down through the water to try to gauge how firm the bottom is before I go in.

On this occasion I spent ages dashing from one side of the river to the other because the swan was determined not to be

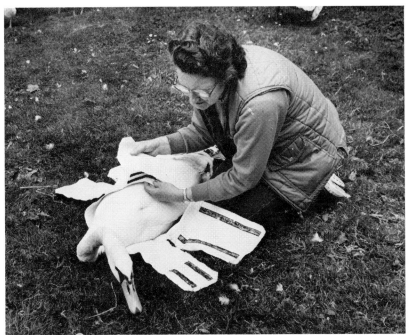

Putting on a swan jacket.   A.G.

caught; once the bird realises your intention, it becomes even more elusive than usual. As time went on various people became interested, and a sewage disposal lorry driver, calling back and forth nearby to offload down into the main sewer, gave me a weight to tie on the end of the rope to fling across the water, and then since a rope alone was not sufficient to stop the swan diving beneath and getting away, I dashed home to take down our net curtains and threadle them along the rope as a deterrent. Imagine my husband's surprise when arriving home that evening to find no net curtains at the windows (he knew it was unlikely I had taken them down for washing!), but perhaps not at all surprised to hear I had put them to a much better use for the swan. The end of the river ran into the canal so the bird kept dashing back and forth. Luckily I managed to divert a friendly traffic warden along the towpath whence the swan kept disappearing, and during this frustrating episode I had to smile seeing the various lovely people who tried to help – definitely a mad swan chase; looking back, one of many.

In those days I could not afford a pair of waders, so I regularly filled my wellingtons up while wading about, and requiring assistance to get them off was the order of the day, because they got stuck on my feet with the suction of the water. However, they say everything comes to those who wait, and one day I was delighted when visiting Watford to find a clothing store was having a sale of fire-damaged stock, and upon investigating discovered way down in a cardboard box a pair of waders marked £7.99. Waders were usually around £48 a pair, so I took them to the cash desk and was even more pleased when I was told that since it was the end of the sale I could have them for £3.99. Even more of a bargain – wading about in water up to the thigh line is not to be recommended without adequate footwear.

There are times when having travelled some distance I find my journey unnecessary, but this is inevitable when several people have called for help from different sources, and on some occasions the swan is all right anyway. Once home in the sanctuary, usually via the vet's surgery, I have a number of sheds to house the patients, and these sheds have to be kept clean with shavings and straw changed regularly. My husband gets bags of shavings from a local wood yard, and these days we buy the straw once a year from a farmer straight off the field at harvest time and store it in another building. Used bedding has to be scraped up and barrowed away, and disinfectant powder and sprays employed against infection and infestation.

An efficient washing machine is important to cope with dozens of dirty towels and bandages, not to mention numerous items of clothing which get soiled whilst handling the birds, supplemented by a good tumble dryer, especially after an unexpected dip into a river or lake. Recently, we had electricity installed down the garden which is a great help when dealing with birds arriving during the hours of darkness. A reliable motor vehicle is, of course, the hub of operations, and needs to be large enough to carry loads of food from the mill, not to mention the odd half dozen swans. I have to reach some pretty inaccessible places whilst rescuing, where there is no help if the car lets me down. I have to rely on a 1979 Peugeot 504 estate which has been a marvellous workhorse with the benefit of new doors and tailgate, general maintenance and servicing, but will not go on for ever, and then the rescue service will cease since I have no money for another.

Within the sanctuary there is a small pond for the birds to keep fit and their feathers waterproof, surrounded by a concrete edge and stones – unfortunately, ducks love to poke about and paddle in mud, thereby gradually encroaching across good pasture. My husband carries out maintenance work on fences and sheds to keep foxes out, and is very competent at wielding a long pole with a net at the end to reach down into weirs, etc. for stranded birds. He also has a telescopic swan hook which reaches a long way across water. When not working as a woodwork contractor, since someone has to earn enough to feed a wife, family and swans, Terry is handy at helping to tube-feed swans, and remove the numerous fishing hooks and line when the birds are too badly damaged to untie at the water's edge and free straight away. I certainly could not manage to launch a rowing boat on my own – he skulls along while I try to grab the swan. Once he was going up river on his own to a shot swan and was suddenly confronted by a length of barbed wire across the water – it was dusk and not visible – thank goodness, some instinct gave him a second to bob down underneath it – and having persuaded the swan to flutter down river to the weir upon which I was balanced, I was able to seize hold and clamber up the bank.

This swan, having been shot, had crashlanded and sustained brain damage, and his treatment was long and arduous. He was a two-year old bird and could not stand without support. He fed well, and took an interest in what was going on around him – we named him Rockefella – he was suspended in a cradle constructed from rubber supports to give him as much movement as possible, and every hour I lifted him for walking exercise; he was given extra drugs and food supplements, and eventually started to move around on his own and graze. Imagine my disappointment, therefore, when one morning I opened the door of his shed, and found him dead. A post-mortem revealed he had died of heart failure. Together we had tried so hard, but it was not meant to be.

Keeping records.   *H.K.*

Unfortunately, rescue and treatment of all the birds involves a certain amount of paperwork and record-keeping, but I am lucky to have a knowledge of business practice, book-keeping and typing which means I fit this in and around all the other activities as time permits. In all financial matters I like to know exactly how much money is available to meet expenses so that I do not get into debt. Sometimes when I am down to the last bag of grain and I know I cannot afford another, I worry that everything may grind to a halt, but somehow or other something always turns up to save the day. It may be a donation, no matter how small, it helps, or occasionally someone turns up with corn. I am a firm believer that if you are meant to do something in life and you are doing it for the right reasons, you will receive the help required.

Chapter 6

LEAD POISONING

For years lead poisoning was the biggest problem we had to tackle in swan rescue. Even in 1987 the Summer saw more lead poisoning cases on the Thames, and a whole flock of swans, built up with enormous dedication, was decimated – some had as many as 50 pieces of lead in their gizzard, and half a dozen can be lethal. People thought that, because legislation had been passed, the lead problem had disappeared overnight but this is not the case – there is always the discarded lead from many, many years lying on waterbeds which is still picked up by swans, especially as the water levels are falling. They feed on submerged vegetation and consume grit daily which is held in a muscular organ called the gizzard. There it is ground down, but the lead is relatively soft and is absorbed into the blood system and thence carried around the body, damaging various other organs and body processes, such that paralysis soon sets in. The gizzard ceases to work, but the swan continues to feed. Food builds up, the neck falls back and soon death occurs; and this whole process only takes three weeks. Not only do we lose adult birds, but cygnets are born with inherited high lead levels and never reach maturity. A bird with lead poisoning is indeed a sick fellow – his breath is foul and his motions stink. Sometimes tube-feeding is a necessity, plus injections with a chelating agent twice daily to neutralise the lead held in the body. Some vets also have an endoscope which enables lead to be removed gradually from

Tube feeding a paralysed swan.   A.G.

the gizzard if a large quantity of weights and swivel hooks are revealed by x-ray. I do not like sliding a tube down the back of a swan's throat – their beautiful black liquid eyes gaze at me, not understanding I am desperately trying to save their life. After a few days' care and treatment I am so pleased when I watch a sick swan get to his feet, legs shaking like mad. Shortly he will take one or two steps forward, he will be grazing, then he will head for the pond to get his feathers back into shape, his neck will straighten up, and then I know he is on the road to recovery. In some cases, after three weeks or so, a bird begins to fall back and he starts to dribble, then I realise that despite having made an initial recovery the extent of the poisoning is so great that now the bones are letting go of absorbed lead, and he is literally slipping away from life.

One such case was a beautiful adult swan rescued from the canal locally. He seemed to get better more quickly than another poisoned swan admitted the same day but he started to deteriorate and I took him back to the vet. Other drugs were prescribed and he started to pick up again. Then, despite having started to graze, he could not stand, so I gave him healing. He sat on my lap in the shed so quietly, and for the first time rested his beak against the back of first one hand then the other. He had been with me six weeks. In the evening I carried him up to the house and he lifted his head on the way up the garden for a last look at the lake. I tried healing again indoors, but then having spread one wing out, he lifted his head in a swinging movement and fell back against me; I laid his head along his back and he closed his eyes for ever. Each bird during treatment becomes part of my life, and recovery gives me great joy, so the only thing to combat the desolation felt when a swan dies is the rescue and rejuvenation of another, the anticipation of returning him to the wild and the joy of reunion with his own environment.

'I really am trying to get better'.   D.S.

Although the problem of fishermen's lead has not entirely disappeared, the other source of lead is from gunshot discharged over waters where birds breed and live, and also over adjacent countryside. There is a move afoot to outlaw the use of leadshot; however, it is said that the alternative steel shot shortens the life-span of a gun barrel, although it has been used in the United States for some time. Meantime, recently I took in an adult swan with approximately thirty pieces of lead gunshot in the gizzard, his neck all fluffed up and yellow, weighing no more more than a puff of cottonwool – too poisoned to save – and whilst the debate continues, more swans die.

Differences between healthy and sick or lead poisoned swans

Healthy	Sick

Eye
Bright and alert

Eye
Narrow, sleepy-looking

Neck
Sleek feathers

Neck
Fluffy feathers

Neck
Graceful curve or held straight

Neck
Kink at base of neck or resting on back

Wings
Held up close to body

Wings
Drooping down side of body

Tail
Straight out behind

Tail
Begins to curve up

Feeding
feeds readily

Feeding
Not enthusiastic.
Drinks constantly and shakes head – opens and closes beak, becomes isolated from other swans. Shaky legs on land. Watery green or black motions.

Part 2

Swan Tales

'A copper engraving named 'Survivors' by Laura Boyd. The swans are
Houdini and Princess along the river Gade at Croxley Green.

Chapter 7

SWANS IN GENERAL

Swans probably became established centuries ago by monks keeping them for food – they were farmed in this country from the twelfth century when cygnets were taken away at three months, kept in pits and fattened for Christmas and special feast days. They became associated with the monarchy, and Edward IV decreed that, with the exception of royal sons, only freeholders of land above a certain value could own and mark swans; all others belonging to the Crown. So in those days there were no wild Mute swans. A Swan Master and deputies were appointed to divide up and mark cygnets between owners before they could fly after breeding, and this custom is continued today on the river Thames in July when the cygnets have their bills marked with one notch for the Dyers and two notches for the Vintners, Crown swans remaining unmarked. Today the Queen only exercises her rights to swans on certain stretches of the Thames.

It is usual for swans to live and breed around the same area unless something happens to prompt them into leaving and flying to waters new. Recently one of the juvenile swans ringed at my sanctuary has turned up in Newcastle under Lyme. It is thought that the swan is the world's heaviest flying animal, and they make a special music with their pulsating wings as they fly overhead. This is a sight our forebears would not have seen, since swans' wings were pinioned by amputating the last section of one wing, thereby making the bird too unbalanced to take off.

It is uncommon to find Mute swans nesting in a colony, and one of the few is at Abbotsbury, Dorset, on the river Fleet. They are able to survive in salt water because they have glands above their eyes to extract salt taken from the bloodstream and excreted through their nostrils. The inland swans are happiest when feeding on water, and having 25 neck vertebrae, more than any other bird or mammal, they are well able to reach plants and roots a metre beneath the water. They love to eat various soft grasses such as eel grass; the parents pull up vegetation for the cygnets to eat, thereby dislodging water boatmen and beetles, etc., and they also paddle their feet to bring food particles to the surface. An adult swan is estimated to need 4lbs of fresh grass every day. When very young the little cygnets love to hitch a lift from their parents and climb up between the wing tip and tail. When rescued, like ducklings, they are great climbers, and lose no time in escaping from hands to shoot up and tuck in around neck and shoulders.

Most parts of the country have regular flocking areas, and nowadays it is not unusual to see a Black swan, originally from Australia and New Zealand, and the close cousin of the Mute swan, living in the same place, and apparently they have been known to breed and produce hybrid young. There have been one or two Black swans in the wild around here, and I have one living on the lake. Some time ago there were two on Startops Reservoir at Tring, and one at Rickmansworth Aquadrome. I have been called out to sick Black swans in private collections, and this is where they are most commonly seen, and whence they escape.

Although swan numbers fell so dramatically in the 1970s, the population has since steadily increased, especially in Scotland where their lives are not so much at risk. A recent survey carried out by The Wildfowl and Wetlands Trust and The British Trust for Ornithology indicates the swan population is still increasing, and the current population in Britain is around 25,700, though the work put in by rescue agencies concerned at the drastic decline has been a major factor in their survival. If you want to know more about swans you should join The Wildfowl and Wetlands Trust who specialise in conserving wildfowl and their wetland habitats and have seven centres you can visit, the most well-known being at Slimbridge, Gloucestershire.

Chapter 8

TELLING TALES

I spend many hours travelling around the surrounding towns
and villages giving talks to every type of group where people
meet together, some associated with wildlife, such as the
RSPB, RSPCA and conservation societies, others of a general
nature, such as Rotary Clubs, Women's Institutes, National
Association of Women's Clubs, Church meetings, not
forgetting the clubs organised by volunteers for the benefit of
people struck down by ill health who are unable to get out
and about. Sometimes I find myself addressing several
hundred people, as in the case of The National Trust, and on
other occasions the audience is much smaller, but they all say
they had no idea of the work put in to rescue and treat swans
in trouble, and how much they have enjoyed hearing about
my activities. I also visit many schools, and it always
stimulates their interest if I am able to take a suitable patient
with me, particularly a cygnet, because when it is fully grown,
ringed and released into the wild, they can go and see how it
is getting on; they know the name it was given in the
sanctuary and it becomes a special friend. I stress the
importance to children and adults alike of picking up and
taking home any discarded line and hooks, etc., also ring
pulls from drinks cans and elastic bands which can get fixed
over ducks' bills and necks.

Having emphasised the serious side of swan care, I then try
to include one or two items about the swans living close by,

which audiences find particularly interesting, and it is for this reason I have been asked to write a book for the people who wanted me to stay and tell them more, but time never allows. I feel it is not always what I say but how I say it that makes people laugh when I am relating rescue tales, and if they have listened, learned and been taken out of themselves into what they previously did not know about and enjoyed hearing of the lighter moments, then I feel I have achieved something worthwhile.

After Mr and Mrs Swan left our lake their place was taken by Muscles and Mary Ann, and their initial venture into parenthood was amusing at first. Late in the breeding season when other birds were actually hatching, I noticed Mary Ann standing on the lakeside at the other end of the bridge across the river looking down behind her. Upon investigation I saw she had laid an egg and was kicking it about as though uncertain where it had come from and what she should do with it. The reeds along the waterside had deteriorated too much to use for nesting material, so I dashed away in the car to fetch some straw, stopping on the way for petrol at the local garage. I told the girl who served me where I was going, and with great alacrity she dashed inside to the till and said, 'Quick, we have an emergency – it's a maternity case!' So I returned home and gave Mary Ann some straw; we found one or two other eggs along the lake, and they were all duly rolled into the nest, and sitting began in earnest. Everything proceeded well until one morning, twenty-one days later, we looked out of our window and neither bird was on the nest. We hurried down to see what had happened and saw all the eggs gone, and since there were no signs or smell of the fox we presume an egg collector had stolen them. It was a sad sight to witness the distress of Muscles and Mary Ann, and in due course they left the lake. The next year they found a more secluded site and hatched two cygnets, and after that they went down to Bourne End, near Berkhamsted, and hatched five cygnets, until one night three disappeared, probably eaten by foxes; the following year they hatched four babies and lost one down a lock in the canal. Most years something happens to one or other of the swan families; sometimes the cygnets die when two week old or so, having used up the yolk with which they were hatched and not been able to feed properly. If the pen knows the cygnet is weak or faulty, she will abandon it, but the youngsters do tend to get lost and that is where a swan sanctuary comes in useful.

Chapter 9

BROADWATER

One May evening I was called out locally to a swan which had been beaten up by a big resident cob living at Water End, near Hemel Hempstead, and had come off the worse for wear. As usual, the injured bird was not very accessible, and I had to climb over a five-bar gate and make my way through brambles and weeds across a swampy area to reach him. I picked him up from the edge of the water, watched by an audience hanging over the bridge railings, but by the time I reached the gate again, everyone had disappeared or so I thought. It was difficult trying to climb back over the gate holding the swan and trying not to fall or lose the run of my rescue paraphernalia, but I had succeeded, when suddenly a nun materialised out of the dusk and offered me some brandy. I thought I must be hallucinating, and whether the brandy was for the swan or swan rescuer I never ascertained! However, the bird was very shaken and I wasted no time getting it home, where after a period of rest it was fit again, and released. Some three months later I was called out to Boxmoor where a swan had flown into the side of a building and although I responded to the call immediately, I was too late; the body was still warm, a huddled heap in the car park, but beyond help, having died in the few minutes it took me to arrive. I recognised him, and by the ring number was able to confirm it was the lovely fellow I had released so joyfully that year, Broadwater.

I was to meet Sister Mary, the kind nun who had offered me help, on another occasion. It was the Autumn and I was due to attend a presentation evening after two local ladies, Nadine Olery and Nina Cole, had worked very hard to raise funds to be divided between the swans and dog rescue. About an hour before I left home, Sister Mary called to say that before it got dark she had seen a swan lying near the river in a field underneath power cables at Water End. We arranged to meet and she said she knew the best way through the sea of deep mud, where the cows stood, to reach the river. Unluckily she missed her bearings in the dark, and, dressed in habit and wellies, went sprawling over in the watery gunge. She could not get to her feet again as it was so slippery, and tried to crawl up one of my arms to stand up, but before she could get upright, she swung around and went splosh on her back. By this time things were getting desperate – the wind was howling and blew away my cries for help, I was slithering around trying to grab her and I could not even have the satisfaction of a few good swear words – what does one say when slipping and sliding around in such atrocious conditions trying to rescue a nun? However, the Lord was on our side, and eventually I managed to pull her upright, and we clung to each other, continuing on our way to the poor swan. Unhappily, by the time we reached the bird it was well and truly dead and relieved of its head, probably by Mr Fox. I picked up the corpse, put it in a plastic bag, and we set off on our hazardous return journey to the stile, swan under my one arm and nun under the other, and I bet somebody upstairs was having a good laugh. Having got over the stile and walked back to the car parked under a lamp, I was horrified to see Sister Mary's habit covered in a really thick layer of mud. It was not her week, as she told me that a few days previously a motorcyclist in London had knocked her over and she was only just getting over that. I was worried about her and took her home to her cottage nearby. Next morning I called to offer help with the laundry, but she was up and about and the washing was already on the line. What a wonderful lady.

Chapter 10

ALL IN A WEEK'S WORK

Saturday morning is usually busy with family coming and going, breakfast to cook, and plans to be made for the weekend. A ring at the front door can set the day rolling to herald a lady clutching a tiny duckling she has found in the water gardens being attacked by other birds. It has sustained a cut head and a twisted neck, but it does not look as though I can do much except put him in the airing cupboard in a box, where he seems to respond, and even takes some food. After a few hours he is squeaking, but later goes quiet again and starts throwing his neck back, which is a sign of impeding death. It is always sad to have to tell people who have brought such birds into care that they have died, but female mallard ducks have several families a year, unlike swans, to balance the high mortality rate.

On Sunday we decide the weather is good and perhaps we can release five swans/cygnets raised together. Moses, abandoned in the river Ver at St. Albans soon after hatching in May, spent several days sculling up and down crying for his mother, but to no avail until a concerned resident called me. I drove over straight away and when I found him scooped him up in a landing net, and cradled him in my arm whilst returning to the car – in gratitude for which he filled up my pocket with a great quantity of droppings which I did not actually notice until I plunged in my hand to fetch out the car keys. One of the joys of animal rescue! It soon became

'Moses, a cygnet rescued from the river Ver at St. Albans, growing up in the sanctuary. D.S.

apparent that he was poisoned and very weak and he ended up in the airing cupboard as well. Eventually he progressed into the bedroom, and one morning I woke up and heard him stomping around, having escaped; I reached out of bed and scooped him up next to me, so imagine my husband's despair upon waking to find me cuddling little Moses, 'Oh my God, she's got a swan in bed now!' – obviously the final straw. It was not long before he was able to go down the garden into a shed with the other swans, and was reared together with a tiny duckling also found in St. Albans, and named Albert by the lady who brought him here, and these two birds were always to be found together, although eventually Albert took off across the river to the lake as the call of the wild became stronger, after which he only popped back and forth for food.

August had seen the admission of a large cygnet, Sinbad, hatched by Mr and Mrs Waitrose in Apsley. He was in serious trouble, having become entangled in fishing line with a large hook embedded in his leg which had become infected; he had also torn the web of one foot. Several operations were performed by Jim Mason at Johnson, Daniels and Partners, and eventually healing was complete. Mr and Mrs Waitrose had already lost one cygnet, wrapped around and drowned in fishing line the previous week. Sinbad became friends with another cygnet around his size from Kings Langley, the 'offspring' of Dennis and Maggie who live at the back of the Old Red Lion, and they are looked after by Hazel and John Welch. This youngster was admitted with eye damage, and hook plus line down his throat, and an x-ray revealed he had also swallowed some small pieces of lead. Treatment was put in hand and in due course 'Horatio' got better, but was blind in one eye. Soon after John called me out to a cygnet wandering along the A41 in the morning rush hour outside a local garage, so I brought it home for observation and name it Pilling after the garage. Just prior to this I was asked to come to a blood-stained adult swan injured in a road accident at Apsley and found one wing torn away from the body. The next day I drove to the vet's where Chris Sander stitched it back. This bird I call Albion after the pub near by.

So we made sure all these birds were ringed, wrapped them in their jackets and drove to the lake chosen for the release. That night it poured with rain, but, checking the next morning, they were all together and settling down quite happily.

Next evening a call from another local fishery to a swan which had flown into an overhead electricity cable, and was lying injured on the edge of their lake. Dusk was falling as I climbed over yet another five-bar gate and walked slowly around until I could find the bird. Meanwhile, the heavens opened and the rain poured down accompanied by thunder and lightning. I managed to seize the bird before it could slither down the bank, and wrapped it carefully in a towel to stem the flow of blood. I negotiated my way over a wobbly plank of wood between two ponds and, soaked to the skin, eventually made it back to the car. After all this, the swan died in a few days as the pectoral muscles had died off, and it could not be stitched together again.

Releasing a cygnet, and tucking his head under his wing, then he gets to his feet in his own time, and walks calmly into the water. Location: Rickmansworth Aquadrome. B.G.

On Tuesday I was very sad to find one of my swan friends floating dead in the canal. I had named her Kara, and every year she had been coming down the river accompanied by her brood of youngsters, but we never saw her husband. To watch Kara one year teaching eight cygnets to fly was magic. She swam to one end of the lake, putting four youngsters to the side and bidding the other four to come and wait behind her, then she would tell them to do as she did and run away from them on the top of the water, 'lifting off' for a short flight, then alight again on the water before reaching the other end of the lake, and they would copy her. After this it was time for the other four to take a turn, and soon she had introduced them all to the art of flight. She was a great swan, such a gentle creature, returning year after year accompanied by her various families, toiling up and down the garden for something to eat, a drink and a sit in the sun, knowing they were all safe here.

On Wednesday, driving around the notorious roundabout in Hemel Hempstead, consisting of a number of mini roundabouts surrounding a main roundabout with a river flowing through it, there on the grass of the big roundabout is the filthiest, tattiest swan I have ever seen. His neck is laid back, and he looks very ill. I find somewhere to park the car, and investigate. He is dribbling like mad, and I gather him up under my arm and plunge across several streams of traffic rushing in all directions and pop him into the car. Enteritis is diagnosed, and treatment put in hand.

Come the evening, another call to the big cob at Great Gaddesden; he is very fierce and has even been known to attack cars crossing the bridge. This time his victim is lying at the edge of the road, a juvenile swan, who is brought into care, and later released.

On Thursday another tiny duckling arrives, found on the aforementioned 'magic roundabout', left abandoned but noticed as being there a long time so a lady brought him here, and I put him in a budgie cage with a feather duster for a foster mother and christen him Zebedee as he becomes more and more bouncy. He thrives, reaches maturity and joins Tinker, Tailor, Soldier and Sailor, a selection of other rescues on the lake.

Zebedee, a duckling abandoned in the middle of 'The Magic Roundabout' in Hemel Hempstead at a few hours old, who has grown up and still lives on the lake at the sanctuary.   P.W.

In between these sort of happenings there are sheds and pond to be cleaned out, dishes washed, treatments dispensed, visits to the vet, trips to the Mill at Tring for food every week, records to be brought up-to-date, letters written, callers at the sanctuary, a television programme to prepare for, the Press and radio appointments, bric-à-brac to collect, sort and price for stalls to raise funds, and all the time the telephone never stops ringing. Apart from this I do the shopping, cooking, washing, ironing, housework now and again, help my husband with his business, walk the dogs, and the rest of the day is my own! Except when I have to go out and give talks in the evening.

Chapter 11

HOUDINI AND PRINCESS

One year I was called out several times to swans in distress on the Grand Union Canal at Croxley Green. This pair had been nesting regularly on an island in the canal and hatched eight cygnets, but only four were still alive; then the cob died from lead poisoning, followed by the pen falling sick, and in addition breaking a wing. To rescue her we launched our little rowing boat to reach the island, from which she was taken aboard and brought into the sanctuary for a long period of treatment and nursing. The youngsters, who were quite large by then, were adopted by an 'auntie' swan and as time went on moved away, especially when another pair arrived to set up home. Joan Cook, who lives alongside the canal and has always taken a great interest in all the birds whilst walking her dog, called me out again when the male of the pair fell sick. At the vet's it was found he had been shot in the head and neck and had a large, rotting hole under his tongue. But there was life in the old soul yet, since he fought to get out of his jacket in the back of the car and I had to stop to wrap him up again before continuing the journey. I found myself comparing him to Houdini, he was such an escape artist, and this became his name.

Treatment was put in hand – antibiotics, cleansing of the wound, and tube-feeding, and he lived to see another day. He was returned to his territory and set up home with the beautiful female, christened Princess by Joan. From that time I have been back and forth when they needed help. On one

Houdini and Princess – a reunion after Princess, a one-footed pen, had been in care. M.Y.

occasion she was noticed to have a leg injury, and to Houdini's disgust I arrived and carried her off for x-ray. He shunted along in the water very worried about her. Unfortunately, the injury was fairly long-standing, and treatment was not possible, so she returned to Houdini very quickly. Not long afterwards it was observed that the foot on the damaged leg was withering away, and eventually the whole foot had gone, and the end of the stump healed over. She continued to live with Houdini and they bred several families, and she was able to take off from the water to fly. I had several enquiries from people noticing she had lost her foot, and once she landed on the Croxley Business Centre, hitting a car and ending up sitting in muddy roadworks. I was able to reassure the men finding her she had not lost her foot in the process, but brought her home suffering from shock. Very soon she was up and stumping around the sanctuary, and I took her back home again. Houdini was so pleased to get her back again, and practically pulled her out of my arms as I lowered her into the canal.

In Spring 1991 they had started nest building on the usual

site when they were interrupted by a stronger pair of swans seeking to take over the territory. Princess had already laid two eggs, but she and Houdini were driven away. Houdini was very battered, and when he and Princess met up he returned to do battle once more but again came off the worse for wear, and they retreated to the nearby river Gade, but did not nest. The pair of swans who took over the island became known as Nobby and Jezebel, and hatched half a dozen cygnets, but rejected two after a couple of weeks; maybe their 'squeak' was different, so they came into care, all greasy, followed by another cygnet found along the river Gade the next week.

That Autumn Houdini was noticed philandering with another female, Molly, a swan rescued a few years ago in the Stanmore area, and Princess was found wandering over a local bridge looking very poorly. Her stump was damaged, and she had swallowed fishing debris. I took her in for nursing and released her as soon as possible back to where Houdini was now loitering along near the original island nest, whilst Nobby and Jezebel were away down the canal at the Marina, where they are known as Henry and Henrietta. So another joyful reunion took place but, alas, short-lived. Back came Nobby and Jezebel, battle commenced and Houdini and Princess were defeated again. They became separated, then Princess returned, to be rejected by Houdini. The final tragedy was when Princess moved to Cassiobury Park in Watford, further down the water, where one sad January day in 1992 she was found dead on the edge of the river, having been attacked by an animal. Houdini is now living in the same area, and has taken another mate.

Chapter 12

BIG BILL

My favourite swan of all is Big Bill. He first came to my attention for rescue when an adult cob living at the back of the local paper mill. He constructed a nest from old bits of paper and wire, and he had thrived there for some time with the thinnest wife in the world. Prior to rescue he had a reputation for sitting slap bang in the middle of the tow path on the canal, and generally behaving in a threatening manner to all and sundry. However, his life nearly came to an abrupt end when I was called out by British Waterways in 1985, and, arriving at their Apsley depot, found him regally seated on a cushion, unable to walk. I brought him home, but it was Sunday and I could not get him x-rayed until the next morning. He was poisoned and paralysed, and very sick indeed. His wife was nowhere to be found, so perhaps she had already succumbed and died. Treatment was started and recovery was slow, until one day he struggled to his feet on wobbly legs and fell down again. I was so pleased to see this, and it was not long before he stood more firmly and took his first steps forward.

Soon after this I was asked to go to Moor Park where a beautiful pen lived, called Jemima. She was the oldest swan I had come across, twenty-three years at least. Originally placed on the pond with two other cygnets, both of whom were thought eventually to have been caught by the fox, only Jemima had survived. She had never sought to leave her home, which was very wise, since it is the only water where no

A likely liaison - Bill and Jemima　　　　　　　　　　　　　　*R.N.*

fishing is allowed. Jemima was having trouble with one leg, so came into the sanctuary for treatment, and as she recovered I noticed she and Bill were attracted to each other. So when they were both fit I took them to Jemima's pond, and the release went well, each making ovations to the other as Bill swam around his new home.

My jubilation was short-lived when a few days later, Jenny Sanders, who lives next door to the lake and had called me out to Jemima and has since worked terribly hard organising a garden fête to raise funds for Swan Care, telephoned to say Jemima had chased Bill off and he was now reposing on a shallow area of water on the nearby golf club. Very gallantly Jenny persuaded a friend to drive her to collect Bill, and took him back to Jemima. Then he went missing again. This time I had a call out to a swan on the canal at Rickmansworth, festooned with fishing tackle. I set off through lanes and fields, ending up in a farmyard at least six inches deep in mud through which I waded to reach the canal, where I found that the bird was Bill. After this it was obvious Jemima was destined to be an old maid, and Bill was found another home on a lake near Moor Park, and he was far from my mind when I got a call from a lady at Oxhey telling me about an oil-covered swan wandering around a local football pitch, until I arrived and found the filthy specimen standing between the goalposts was Bill, having crawled out of the nearby river Colne which was heavily polluted with oil. Home we came, and the lengthy process of cleaning up oily feathers was put in hand, together with internal treatment, since he had been trying to clean himself up and had swallowed oil as well.

After this I decided to put him on a canal again, but at Tring, where a stretch of water had become vacant after the original bird had flown into cables and died. Here Bill found a wife, and together they nested and hatched four cygnets – after a few weeks the cygnets all died one morning from botulism. I crawled down a culvert to the last live cygnet when I heard they had started to die, and brought it home in a desperate bid to save it, but despite everything did not succeed. The following September I was asked to come to a tributary of the canal past Heygates Mill at Tring where a swan was lying in the weed. I raced out straightaway and found poor Bill lying paralysed yet again. More visits to the vet, more treatment – we prayed for a miracle, and our wish was granted. At the end of October I set off with Bill in the back of the car. I stopped at the British Waterways yard at Bulbourne to ask if they had seen Mrs Bill recently. She had not been sighted. I drove to another part of the canal and spoke to some other British Waterways workers on one of their boats near the Wendover Arm; one man said he had seen Mrs Bill flying away some days before. Undeterred I unloaded Bill from the car and decided to walk along the waterside, feeling Mrs Bill might be about, and on rounding a bend was delighted to see an adult female swan up ahead. I called to her, and she answered, whereupon Bill wriggled like mad to get out of his bag. I stopped and untied him, and he stood on the towpath, stretched himself to his full height, flapping his wings and walked towards his wife, 'talking' to her; he slid down the bank into the water and glided quickly towards her. They met full on, pressing their breasts together, heads side by side, entwining necks, totally absorbed in their reunion. I stood alone on the bank watching them, a lump in my throat, privileged to watch this magic moment – this is what all the hours of work and worry are about.

However, the saga of Bill was to continue further. In March

1990 came another call to Bill – he was fetched in and x-rayed – more swallowed fishing weights – more treatment, but he recovered and was returned as soon as possible to Mrs Bill, who since it was the mating season had been receiving the attention of Mr Tom, a big cob living on Marsworth Reservoir nearby, who had recently lost his wife. So this time Mr Bill returned to find his wife dallying with another cob and unable to make up her mind as to which swan she preferred. She commuted between canal and reservoir, and Tom started beating up poor Bill, and the season passed with no nesting. Tom did not like any of the other females on the adjacent Startops Reservoir enough to settle down, and Mrs Bill obviously has that *je ne sais quoi*, making her irresistible.

1991 started off with a further call to Bill who was reported tied up with hook and line; I pulled him aboard a boat and brought him back for x-ray. After treatment I took him back again, and he and Mrs Bill got together that year and a nest was built along the Wendover Arm, and sitting commenced, but unfortunately nothing came of it. 1992 has seen Bill up on Startops Reservoir on his own, nothing like the bird he used to be, so I do not know what the next episode will be.

Chapter 13

TOM

Having mentioned Tom in the last chapter I will tell his story now. In August 1988 I admitted what had once been a huge cob swan from Tring Reservoir but was now a paralysed bundle of feathers, bleeding from the mouth, and completely unable even to raise his head. The fishermen who had seen him had been reduced to tears by his plight – I wish all fishermen could be brought to the realisation of how swans suffer. I really doubted whether I could save him, but set off to Watford to the vet for x-ray and advice. Poor Tom was really 'splat' for the next few days, and visitors to the sanctuary stood weeping to see him.

The following weekend my friend, Anne Duvall, held a garden fête in aid of various charities at her canalside cottage in Berkhamsted. Since Chris Sander had suggested I should take more of my patients out of the sanctuary so people could see what a sick swan looks like, I took poor Tom along and sat him on the grass in the shade with food and water. He aroused much interest, and criticism for keeping him alive, although I told these people many swans come into care in a terrible state, but with treatment they do recover.

I think if ever a swan was meant to get better it was Tom, as so many people were wishing him well again, and that day he lifted his head and neck for the first time, and at night when placed in his shed he stood up and took two steps forward, and after that began to recover. Intensive treatment continued

Tom and Molly, mature swans having been rescued and treated on their way to release at a private lake in Stanmore.
R.N.

and he made such good progress that within a few weeks he was released, with a pen with whom he had made friends in the sanctuary, to a private lake at Stanmore, but soon after they went their separate ways and he flew to Marsworth Reservoir where the following Spring he and his wife produced a family of four cygnets.

The next year his mate died, and he began flying from one reservoir to the other and also became acquainted with Mrs Bill. Soon afterwards I released Bill again and Tom set about him, so Bill had to be taken to safety by Pat Thomas and Diana Oughton who live nearby, checking and feeding the swans every day when food is scarce, and let me know when they think a bird needs attention. During the winter of 1991 Bill held his territory along the Wendover Arm and Mrs Bill stayed with him, so Tom continued to live around Marsworth Reservoir until the following Spring when someone rang and told me about a swan sitting on the side. I rang and asked Pat to investigate, and she went out straight away and fetched the bird in, only to find it was Tom, and he died ten minutes later. Les Stocker took the body away, and after post-mortem he found Tom had died of starvation because of a bundle of fishing line down his throat.

Chapter 14

ISAAC

Sometimes I do not actually have to leave the sanctuary to rescue swans since they seem to be directed here by unseen forces, and only need bringing in off the lake or out of the river in case they come to the attention of P19 and Lady, our resident swans. Once they have been in care they know where to return for help. One such case was a cygnet released weeks earlier whom I found early one morning desperately trying to get back into the sanctuary from the riverside. I could see he was seriously injured, dragging a torn leg behind him, covered in maggots. I phoned Chris Sander and drove straight into Watford for help. With great difficulty the wound was eventually cleansed, dressings applied and injections given – we assumed Isaac had been attacked by a fox.

It was Autumn and the weather still warm – I carried Isaac down the garden and put him on the grass, and later in the morning I saw two more cygnets arrive at the bottom of the garden; they were his brothers. I opened the gate and they hurried up to greet him and then sat one on either side, no doubt to encourage him to get better. The Kaltostat dressings applied to this injury were marvellous, and healing quickly took place and hopes of a recovery were raised, until circulation to the foot failed and it became obvious he would lose it. So it was decision time – how could I see a beautiful cygnet condemned to a life of hobbling around on a stump, never knowing his inheritance of freedom in the air and on the water, and constantly at risk when the stump was damaged and infection set in again. So looking back, rightly or wrongly, I asked if I might hold him whilst he was put to sleep, and I was very upset that after six weeks of loving and caring I had to let him go. After this his brothers went on their way, and hopefully are still going strong.

Chapter 15

JOEY

Even if I am called out to a cygnet floating alone on water with no parents nearby, I cannot say there must be something congenitally wrong and it has been deliberately neglected, although it may be nature – in this day and age sickness may be caused for so many reasons. One afternoon in August 1988 I was asked by a lady to go and look at a cygnet in such a situation at Rickmansworth Aquadrome. He was floating aimlessly about, his little head and neck laid right back; he had apparently been like it for days and people passing by had not noticed. I waded out into the reservoir and managed to get hold of him, and drove him to the vet for x-rays. He had six pieces of lead and a ledger weight in his gizzard – prognosis 'very poor'.

I took him home and started treating him; he could feed but not walk. Every morning I expected to find him dead in his shed, but he kept going, and when put out on the grass, shunted himself along to the pond to join the other birds. He was sharing a shed with an adult swan, and one morning I found him standing up and was delighted. But as the day went on he did not join the others on the pond, and at night had not eaten. The following day I could see he was deteriorating, and sat that afternoon holding him on my lap praying he would rally, although I felt he would not; and so he died with his dear little eyes open, so quietly, no fuss – just slipping gently out of his short life of twelve weeks – cruelly foreshortened by a careless fisherman, it was hardly worth struggling out of the eggshell.

He was one of five cygnets rescued that week – all festooned with fishing tackle, and the same day Joey died I was out again in the evening at the river Gade in Croxley catching another little cygnet tied up with line round and round its neck, lead and a hook down the throat. Not a good day since it had started in the morning trying to catch Mrs Tom on Marsworth Reservoir at Tring to the accompaniment of a nearby fisherman, jeering and swearing and urging me to leave the swan to die.

Chapter 16

PEGGY AND FRED

There are many people all over the country to whom swans owe much for their wellbeing. Swans always remain aloof and dominant, except when it comes to food. I suspect there are quite a number of humans who live near water and receive constant calls from swans knocking at their doors and windows. One such couple are Joan and Reg Oughton whose garden is on the side of the canal at Kings Langley. I originally got to know them some years ago when they needed help and advice with cygnets; then one Spring their local adult female swan, whom they named Peggy, decided to move in and nest in their garden. This was no ordinary garden, it was Joan's pride and joy – a prize-winning garden, the subject of many hours of hard work creating a *pièce de résistance*, so imagine the anguish of watching a swan ripping up award-winning specimens and casting them behind and around her to build a nest. I am glad to say that their love for the swans won in the end, and I think they have had much pleasure from their beautiful feathered friends.

So Peggy was allowed to stay, together with her mate, Fred, and, as they were supplied with a quantity of straw to aid the nest building, it was not long before they produced a family. This happy state of affairs continued for another year with the occasional visit from me to sort out various ups and downs concerning parent birds and babies, until one terrible day when Fred was found floating dead in the canal, with Dennis, a cob from the adjoining territory, riding along on top of him lifting him up and down by his neck. We tried for a long time to divert Dennis by throwing him pieces of bread, which he came and ate then rushed straight back to Fred. Eventually I was able to knock him off with a long pole, and pull Fred from the water, by which time he was so heavy I shall never know how I managed to carry him to the car. A post-mortem revealed Fred had been suffering from pneumonia, so probably fell easy prey to Dennis.

Everyone feared Peggy would never breed again, but I reassured them and it was not long before another male swan moved in and a few weeks later she was nest building again. Since then she has had another husband, called Danny, and he has got into trouble several times, requiring rescuing, until sadly in the Spring of 1991 he was one of several swans found dying along that stretch of the canal as a result of ingested fishing weights, swivel hooks, etc. He was so ill that I had to ask Keith Walker, a dedicated swan helper with his wife, Jill, to take Danny to Dot Beeson who runs The Swan Sanctuary at Egham. He was put on an intravenous drip into his leg, but was too far gone, and died that night.

The next night Peggy was robbed of the eggs upon which she was sitting, so she was a very sad sight floating aimlessly up and down her territory wondering what was happening. In the Spring of 1992 Peggy is once more nesting in the same place with a mate who has been called Toby, and seems to be as eccentric as was Danny in that as fast as Peggy is making her nest, he is bent on taking it away again.

I am hoping that life will be more productive for Peggy without too many interruptions from the aforementioned Dennis, who is still living on some water running parallel with the canal behind Waterside in Kings Langley. Dennis and his mate, Maggie, are looked after by some more friends, Hazel and John Welch; here again the swans live and nest at the bottom of a garden so are protected to a certain extent, although the fox is very active in the area. One year we had great excitement when this family of cygnets became separated from Dennis and Maggie by one of the canal locks, and another swan friend, Beverley Huish at Hunton Bridge told me three little cygnets had gone down the canal past her cottage on their own. It turned out one cygnet was still with the parents, and by the time John Welch, Joan and Reg Oughton and I had borrowed Beverley's inflatable dinghy and launched it into the canal where the cygnets had last been sighted, it was dark. John and I crammed into the boat, one at each end, me with a special lamp I have for use at night to leave hands free, which consists of a torch worn around the head as with a miner's lamp, and always brings forth comments from people insinuating I should be going below ground. But despite all efforts we could not find the babies, and abandoned our search until next day. Then Beverley's children located the cygnets and I went out along the canal again, this time in the pouring rain. I managed to catch all three missing babies, popped them into a basket and drove back towards Kings Langley where I found Dennis and Maggie, whereupon Dennis got out of the water and tried to wallop me for stealing his family. Such is swan rescue.

Luckily, friends of the swans such as these abound all

around this area, throughout the three counties I mostly frequent rescuing swans, so I have birds in the sanctuary from Hertfordshire, Befordshire and Buckinghamshire. There are lots of swans around Bedford, and sometimes they arrive via the RSPCA, although one poor cob swan last Spring was beyond help after someone cut his head off and stole the pen's eggs, and every year this happens when egg collectors are about. I have seen the pen battered off the nest by somebody wielding a heavy object, breaking

This swan was shot dead on the river Colne at Watford by a boy with an airgun.
R.N.

her bones, causing her to bleed to death; on other occasions the pen bird has been shot dead. There is now a fine of £1,000 for interfering with a swan, an egg or a nest.

Most towns have a river and a park where everyone may go to see swans, and this is the case in places like Chesham, Bucks., where the swans take flight and land amongst houses, and along country lanes, and cannot take off again because there is not sufficient room to get airborne, or they have injured themselves. Other places have boating and sailing areas inhabited by swans, as in Rickmansworth, or country parks as at Aldenham. But wherever we have water these days we also have the risk of pollution, and this is becoming a big problem.

Chapter 17

OTHER FEATHERED FRIENDS

Since I rescue swans I get asked to come to the aid of all sorts of animals, but I try to restrict my activities to water birds, especially as I am limited by finance, and I think all animal rescue groups have the same difficulty. In my area I am not aware of another swan sanctuary, but I do know of sanctuaries for all sorts of other birds. If a swan call comes in from the Slough area it would be directed to Swan Lifeline run by Tim Heron who has been rescuing swans for years, and is hoping to raise enough money to set up a sanctuary on the river Thames near Eton. As already mentioned Dot Beeson has a large swan sanctuary at Egham. If you need help having found a swan in trouble it is a good idea to telephone your local Police who are best placed to put you in touch with a local source of help should the RSPCA not be able to attend.

It is not unusual for unwanted birds to be dumped in local parks, and prior to being left the unscrupulous owners hack wings so the bird cannot fly home again. I was called upon to take in a bird which had got into such trouble. He was a black Muscovy duck, and after treatment was returned to the local water gardens, but was set upon by the other birds, which is not unusual, so back home he came, and settled down happily on our lake. I named him Sam and he was quite a character. Every morning he would wait over the lake until I called him, then I would put his food on top of the coal bunker and he would launch himself into flight up the garden, and thump down to eat his fill. After his food, he would take a rest and in due course take off again. He was probably quite the ugliest bird I have rescued, and some people do not like Muscovy because of the red skin around their head and back, called caruncles, but once we got used to each other, he seemed to become more handsome since his behaviour was so endearing. I was sorry when one morning my husband found Sam dead on the side of the lake, killed by the fox, so we buried what remained down the garden.

After Sam came Monty, another Muscovy brought in by a lady from the water gardens, very battered and bruised, with an injured leg. Again, not a very appealing specimen but harmless enough, and over the following months he grew splendid new plumage, which he washed in the pond, and became a new bird. He was quiet and friendly, and seemed to enjoy life here. He lived in a chicken shed with various ducks and geese, but one Saturday did not seem like his usual self, he just sat about and by Sunday was worse. He died that night, so Chris Sander did a post-mortem and found that peritonitis killed him. Other Muscovy ducks have come and gone, and I try to get them into a shed at night so the fox does not get them. I had one very ancient black and white Muscovy whom I called Grandad. His shed was adjacent to some garages next door to our garden, and once or twice when letting him in and out, talking to him and saying things like, 'Hello, Grandad' or, 'Goodnight, Grandad', it did occur to me that people putting their cars away might wonder if I had resorted to keeping our Grandad in a garden shed.

Canada geese have been frequent patients at the sanctuary, the first of many being one I named Arthur – he was very ill and considered to be beyond veterinary help; he came with a broken leg and advanced arthritis. He had been dragging himself along on his breast, and had very few feathers. His feet were all curled up and he looked and smelled generally disgusting. I was asked if I would take him into care otherwise he would be put down. So I set off to collect him. When I saw the state of him, I wondered if I was doing the right thing. However, nothing ventured, nothing gained, so I took him away with me, and settled him into a comfortable corner of the shed, and every afternoon I would sit with him on my lap massaging

Arthur, a Canada goose, who was considered beyond veterinary help when admitted, tattered and torn; taken prior to release.   S.C.

his legs with comfrey ointment, working it into the dried up webs until they became supple again. I was not so sure how to tackle his twisted neck which was bowed down across his breast, but every day gently held it slightly straighter and asked in prayer that I might be used as a channel to heal this poor bird, and reassured him that very soon he would be the most beautiful bird in the world. It took a few weeks before he really started to respond, but eventually his feet spread out, he was able to stand again, his neck became almost straight and it was not long then before he was walking about and his feathers grew back.

As time went on he was well enough to go over the lake, and was pleased to get on to a large expanse of water, but unfortunately the resident swan took an instant dislike to him and chased him off across the river, where he was later discovered by neighbours hobbling about, and when I fetched him back again he had a broken toe. He had another spell of care, but it healed and he went back to the lake where he was allowed to settle, and would run up to me whenever I crossed the bridge. The British Trust for Ornithology came along and ringed him, after which he went to live on the canal outside the lake. He was there for a long time, before flying away, probably with a flock of visiting geese. Since this time the Canada geese have become a pest as their numbers are continually increasing, and we have a flock of at least two hundred moving around this district. They have become a native bird now and descend upon our lake with a deafening noise; they have such voracious appetites they strip whole grassy areas of food which otherwise would provide grazing for swans. During the breeding season they have a very successful method of keeping the babies in groups cared for by 'aunties', and this is why they have multiplied so quickly.

I have also had a succession of Embden geese for care and treatment, finding new homes for them as and when possible. Currently we have a small flock of five who live in constant disharmony on and off the lake since there are two ganders and three geese, and the two ganders do not get on together. One white female is known as Hatty since she has a tuft of feathers sticking out from the top of her head, and another brown and white female I call Dolly. In 1989 Hatty started laying eggs all over the place, I never knew where she would be sitting next, even deep in the compost, her head and neck sticking up like a periscope. So I was relieved when she finally settled down in a chicken shed, and continued to lay her eggs

'Follow our leader' - some of my rescued Embden geese.　　　P.W.

in the corner, sitting all day and coming out in the evening to stretch her legs and have a dip in the pond, then Dolly would pop into the shed and take over sitting duties. I thought Dolly was a male since I had seen them mating on the water and decided I might have to re-christen her Boy Dolly, then one evening she was found to have laid a soft egg in the middle of the lawn so it became clear that Dolly had been nipping into the shed every night to lay another egg, and so far there were eighteen in the nest and all infertile. However, the situation was saved when I had three goslings and a cygnet in and tucked them all under Hatty in the evening, removing the old eggs, and in due course Hatty and Dolly became devoted mothers to the new goslings, Pip, Squeak and Wilfred.

I also have a Chinese goose who rules the sanctuary, and makes an awful noise like a creaking gate. He came via the vet's after his wife was killed, and he was admitted for care. When I fetched him from the surgery a nurse asked what type

of bird he was and what I might call him, and looking in his super pen and what he had done to it I suggested 'Who Flung Dung', but having regard for the knob on his head which is really an extension of the bill I conceded that Nobby might be appropriate, and anyway my neighbours have quite enough to put up with, without me running around the garden calling 'Who Flung Dung'! Nobby's best friend is Donald, an Aylesbury duck abandoned at a local school just before Christmas several years back; he has one 'aeroplane' wing, an inherited defect very common amongst birds dumped in parks. At the

'Nobby' our Chinese goose who rules the sanctuary.   S.C.

72

moment I also have a Muscovy duck from another local school which has two 'aeroplane' wings and looks just ready for take-off. The children have named him Hob Nob, after the biscuit of the same name for which he had a particular liking when they were feeding him before I arrived. Nobby rules the roost, and does not like other people getting too close either to Donald or me, and he charges around with his chin on the ground like a hoover; size holds no fear for him, he will run straight up to and over a swan. However, at Springtime Donald's thoughts turn to love, and he is smitten with one of my black labrador dogs, Jacob. Poor Jacob cannot venture down the garden without Donald waddling up and quacking at him, nipping him and following along wherever he goes.

I also have a pair of Aylesbury ducks, but they were hatched last year, and now live together over the lake; their names are Spick and Span, and their special crony is a Welsh Harlequin duck whom I call Look You. At one time I took in a pair of Crested ducks. The drake is jet black and his wife was a light shade of grey; I named them Samson and Delilah, but poor Delilah died suddenly when she developed ovarian trouble during the breeding season.

At one time I had a peacock living here, and it was not long before the whole neighbourhood knew he was living with us. I christened him Percy and despite everything he gave us great pleasure, although when he insisted on sitting outside the aviary at night instead of inside, he did worry me a lot. On a frosty night he would get frozen, and when he jumped down into the garden at dawn, all the bits of ice dropped off him in a shower. His wings had been badly chopped, but he gradually returned to the beautiful bird he once was, and I found him a lovely home with Jane Allan at Berkhamsted. I had hoped he would settle with her white peahen, Precious, but Precious became sick before they could breed, although Jane has another peahen now, so perhaps there will be a happy ending one day. Life has been very quiet since the departure of Percy as one of his main preoccupations was to stand and look at his reflection in our lounge window and call to it. I think the chickens are glad he has gone because he would insist on spreading his tail and making ovations to them, but they were quite unimpressed and just kept on moving, so when he turned round to see what was happening, they had gone.

For a long time I had an Egyptian goose living on the lake with one-and-a-half wings – she had been rescued and lived in the sanctuary whist recovering, but did not enjoy being shut in a shed at night, and finally I let her stay out in the wild. There she was quite happy and came regularly into the garden to feed all the time, and became known as Cleo. I was very

'Cleo', one of several Egyptian geese rescued, once with a broken leg then with half a wing missing, who finally settled on our lake. B.G.

pleased when a male Egyptian goose turned up one Saturday morning until I went down the garden to look at him, and saw he had an enormous yellow, swollen foot instead of a thin red foot, and it was obviously causing him much pain. Eventually that evening I succeeded in enticing him into the river and got hold of him, but when the deadly monofilament fishing line was unwound from his poor ankle, he shook his leg and the foot fell off except for a small piece of skin. An emergency dash to the vet's surgery where Jim Mason and his staff had just cleaned up at the end of another busy day was not guaranteed to make me the most popular client, but they took it all in their stride as usual; they were so kind and efficient, and set about treating and dressing Pharaoh's foot. Home again, where Pharaoh was put in the dining room for peace and quiet in which to get over his ordeal, and for a couple of weeks he did well, and was then transferred to the hospital shed at the top of the garden, until one awful morning when I opened the door and found him dead on the floor. Perhaps the stress of incarceration became too much for him – I have found geese much more difficult to bring through traumas than swans. But I was very disappointed that Cleo had come so close to finding a partner, and yet again fishing line had taken another life.

So life goes on, never knowing who will need help next, and I feel very fortunate to be able to do what I enjoy. I am a free spirit and love the birds which brings much happiness when I see them getting better, and going on their way. If only one or two others are encouraged to make the commitment, the arduous task of writing this book will have been worthwhile – a fulfilled life takes on a new meaning – time is the greatest gift we have, and if you take pleasure in putting each day to good use, you are a millionaire.

Even if you cannot become as committed as I have to swan care you can help them survive by keeping a check on those you see regularly, and report any that seem to be in difficulty to the nearest local authority, or lock-keeper; on the Thames an official swanmarker; the local RSPCA, or the Police have a note of other swan rescue organisations. When notifying these people it is helpful if you can give a ring number, time, place and description of circumstances affecting the swan, and if assistance is not quickly available, it is a good idea to try to 'contain' the swan in an enclosed area such as a yard or garden, or even a garage or alleyway.

Rubbish of all kinds, especially discarded fishing tackle, needs to be collected, and in my area special clean-ups are organised. I try to encourage youngsters to join angling clubs where they are taught the Anglers' Code of Conduct.

As the number of swan territories decline and the quality of their habitat deteriorates they are becoming more and more dependent on us for food, so extra food especially in Winter is much appreciated. They love bread though it is not very good for them, so it is better if they can be given mixed corn, wheat, pellets or flaked maize, and if their pond has become frozen it is essential the ice is broken so they can drink, swim and preen.

Swan rescue charities are always glad to know of safe homes if you know of someone with a suitable large area of free water, and are always glad to receive unwanted bread and/or greens to supplement food supplies.

In the case of my rescue organisation I am very grateful to Johnson, Daniels & Partners of 256 Cassiobury Park Avenue, Watford, Hertfordshire, for collecting silver foil and aluminium cans in aid of the swans. Money raised by coffee mornings, jumble sales, charity stalls, boot sales, sponsored events, etc. all provide a life-line to keep going.

Chapter 18

UPDATE ON SWAN CARE

Life in the swan sanctuary has been hectic since the original publication of this book, and the following is a brief update.

Flotsam and Jetsam
Six cygnets hatched to the first pair of breeding swans in Hemel Water Gardens for fourteen years, giving much pleasure to the hundreds of people watching them every day, but it was sad that four of these babies died by drowning on their second day of life. The remaining two were also washed down a weir but were saved, and I brought them into care, waterlogged and suffering from pneumonia. However, they were treated and survived. I called them Flotsam and Jetsam, and in the Autumn they were released onto a lake. Not long after, one swallowed a fishing hook and I rescued him again, removed the hook and he was soon able to return to the flock with whom he was living.

P19 and Lady
P19, our resident cob, died from gastro-enteritis the day before his mate, Lady, hatched six cygnets in 1993, and the first few days of life for these babies were hazardous because Lady could not carry six young on her back, and once or twice we found a very exhausted cygnet too tired to climb out of the water. I sat out on the lake every night for the first week in case the fox came along and snatched the youngsters. Lady

also stayed awake all night, constantly watching around her, not resting until dawn.

Unfortunately, Lady went looking for P19, and ventured down the river Bulbourne behind the Fishery Inn where she and her family were attacked by a fierce cob living on the canal. I was alerted and went along straightaway, plunging into the river to push the cob back up the bank. At the same time, Lady panicked and thought I was taking her babies away when I was actually pulling them out from behind logs in the river where they were trapped by flood water, but eventually I was able to reunite them up river, and they returned to our lake.

Two days later, she went down river again, and this time the cob succeeded in killing one baby, and another was swept down the adjacent weir and carried away under the canal. After this, Lady reared the four remaining cygnets, staying on her lake until the Spring when she flew away. In June I found her badly injured, lying in the river opposite sewage works at Berkhamsted. Despite intensive treatment, she died a week later. A very special swan – leaving a gap in our lives which will be very hard to fill.

Muscles and Mary Ann

One Monday morning in September, 7.30 am, pouring with rain I received a telephone call from a lady to say she had seen a sick swan on the local rugger field unable to hold its neck up, head rolling around. I rushed along to see what had happened, and by the time I arrived the swan had staggered over to the river and into the water. I crawled down the steep bank and lifted her out. On her leg, she had a white darvic ring, which I have not used for years, so I knew she was an old friend.

Once home I established she was Mary Ann, the mate of Muscles from Winkwell, Bourne End. It was obvious she was poisoned – her wings hung down – one web was torn, she had a growth on one foot and a fishing hook and line in one leg. But it was inside the bottom of her neck about which I was most concerned – she was writhing in agony. I rushed her home and rang the vet, who told me to take her in straight away, but she had already gone into her death throes and died in my arms. I took her body in to Chris Sander for a post mortem and he found that her oesophagus was torn open by a huge fishing hook which was still in her throat. Fresh maggots were in evidence, indicating she had been caught up by a fisherman the day before, who had cut his line and gone home, leaving this most beautiful swan to crawl away from her family and die in torment. If only he had been caring enough to report the incident so that her life might have been saved.

A fortnight later I was notified of another swan at Winkwell who was limping, and when I arrived found a fisherman feeding it, not having noticed a large rusty three-barbed hook protruding from behind the bird's knee joint. The swan was Muscles, the mate of Mary Ann; I pulled him out of the water – he could not stand and was visibly ill. The hook was cut from the decaying leg which had become poisoned, so he was taken to the vet's for x-rays and blood tests. Following treatment he was released, and went on looking for his missing wife.

Just before Christmas, Muscles was attacked by another cob on the canal and was noticed huddling in a rose bush outside River Park flats in Boxmoor. I took him home and arranged to take him in to the vet's the next day, and was very sad to find him dead, spread out on the floor of the shed the next morning. Again a post mortem was performed, revealing an infection in his chest from yet another fishing hook.

So that was the end of a splendid pair of swans, years before their time, subjected during that short life to continual harassment by fishing activities, necessitating my being called out to rescue them and their babies on an average of 3–4 times a week.

Their territory has now been taken over by another young pair of swans I call Adam and Eve. I have already rescued Adam with three fishing hooks down his throat, treated and released him again.

New Patients

It was around this time that a swan rescued from Tring Reservoirs was seen to be throwing his neck about, and x-rays revealed a rusty needle wedged across the bottom of the oesophagus (later identified by fishermen as being the type they use). After removal, the bird was treated with anti-biotics and taken back to Tring.

Christmas Day saw a beautiful male swan killed in our local water gardens following impact with an immovable object, a post mortem showing a broken clavicle.

On Boxing Day a swan brought in from Rickmansworth Aquadrome following head injury, covered the treatment room in blood, such that it looked like an abattoir. The bird was much bothered by a large, soft growth which had developed over one eye, and as the bird preened and rubbed his head around to try and rid himself of the irritation he kept rubbing the skin and making it bleed. So once again, my marvellous vet, Chris Sander, was called into action the next day to remove the growth, which was sent away for biopsy and turned out to be cancerous. However, the swan called 'Stanley' by Neil from the Rickmansworth Ski Club who had rescued him, did live to see another day, and has his freedom again, and so far seems to be keeping well.

Houdini, Nobby and Jezebel
Houdini from Watford, now living in Cassiobury Park, took another mate in 1993, building a nest near the canal, but the eggs became scattered and nothing came of the mating. In 1994 they have nested further from the canal in what we hope will be a safer spot – they have hatched three babies, but I have had differing reports as to what has happened since.

The pair of swans originally known as Nobby and Jezebel who ousted Houdini and his previous wife, Princess, from their island in the canal at Croxley have continued to breed successfully at the same site, and in 1994 they have seven cygnets, spending much time around the Marina at Croxley where they have lots of friends on the boats, especially Theresa Wilson and her husband, John.

Big Bill
My favourite swan, Big Bill, following a very chequered life, spends most his his life of Startops Reservoir at Tring, but has not found another mate with whom to settle down.

Summary
Currently, I rescue an average of two hundred swans yearly, not to mention dozens of cygnets and ducklings. Every Winter

the grass in the sanctuary is worn away, made worse by constant rain which encourages even more beaks to dabble in puddles, but miraculously the grazing is renewed each Spring.

The laborious work of lifting 25kg sacks of food, and lugging bales of straw and bags of shavings to clean out sheds is very tiring, and there are always mountains of towels to wash and dry; the door bell and telephone never stop ringing, and always the fund-raising must continue.

To this end it has been necessary to take part in television programmes, radio interviews, various environmental forums and exhibitions to keep the public informed, and a trip to Buckingham Palace which was really a waste of time.

A feeling of isolation is inevitable since the last fifteen years of swan rescue, twenty-four hours a day, without a day off, has swallowed so much precious time, but reading back over past records, at least I know that the time has been well spent.

My biggest problem is the Grand Union Canal which is a focus for fishermen from far and wide; they arrive in busloads and pour out all along the towpaths. They tell me other waters are becoming polluted, so the problem of swan rescue here is never likely to diminish, seventy-four rescue calls to swans being the average during any one season. However, in the period between August 1993 and August 1994, I have rescued an unprecedentedly high total of 208 victims of coarse fishing tackle pollution. I am constantly wondering what can be done about the irresponsible element among fishermen. Some are aggressive, resent others using the towpath and foul the hedgerows and woodland adjacent to where they fish. Complaints by the general public to the appropriate water authority or fishing club are rarely publicised heavily, as angling is one of the biggest leisure industries in the country and too much money is at stake.

It is a step in the right direction that a Swan Convention has been formed which meets annually in Stratford upon Avon; originally initiated by Councillor Cyril Bennis, it is now run by the National Initiative for Tighter Angling Controls, seeking to bring together all engaged in swan rescue. In 1993 the meeting was attended by Ken Ball, the President of the National Federation of Anglers, Dr Kevin Bond from the National Rivers Authority, and also the Wildfowl & Wetlands Trust.

A Swan Study Group has been set up for some years to collate and discuss information regarding the ringing of swans all over the country, and in 1994 the venue was the Wildfowl & Wetlands Trust centre at Welney, Cambridgeshire.

After this meeting, together with Swan Lifeline from Slough, I was privileged to accept an invitation from the RSPCA group to accompany them back to their new Norfolk Wildlife Hospital at East Winch, near Kings Lynn. This marvellous new unit is equipped with the most sophisticated facilities for the treatment, care and rehabilitation of wildlife casualties. Alison Hutchinson, the Head Nurse, gave us a guided tour during which we met Ian Robinson, the veterinary surgeon leading this dedicated team of workers.

Having carried the burden of wildfowl rescue myself for so long, dare I hope that the need for facilities to be available through a nationally recognised organisation might now be met by the RSPCA, an established charity, who also have a wildlife centre in Somerset. Now we need pressure to be exerted in this direction, so that everybody has a fairly local centre to which they can refer in times of need, instead of being dependent upon the driving force of one person.

Meantime, more swan tales are in progress, so please stay tuned!

WHERE TO VISIT SWANS

Abbotsbury Swannery, Abbotsbury, Dorset.
Tel: Abbotsbury (030 587) 228

The Wildfowl & Wetlands Trust, Slimbridge,
Gloucestershire, GL2 7BT.
Tel: Cambridge, Gloucs. (045 389) 333

and also

The Wildfowl & Wetlands Trust, Mill Road, Arundel,
West Sussex, BN18 9PB.
Tel: Arundel (0903) 883355

Wildfowl & Wetlands Trust, Eastpark Farm, Caerlaverock,
Dumfriesshire, Scotland, DG1 4RS.
Tel: Glencaple (038 777) 200

The Wildfowl & Wetlands Trust, Martin Mere, Burscough,
Ormskirk, Lancashire, L40 0TA.
Tel: Burscough (0704) 895181

The Wildfowl & Wetlands Trust, Peakirk, Peterborough,
Cambridgeshire, PE6 7NP.
Tel: Peterborough (0733) 252271

The Wildfowl & Wetlands Trust, District 15, Washington,
Tyne & Wear, NE38 8LC.
Tel: Washington (091) 416 5454

The Wildfowl & Wetlands Trust, Pintail House,
Hundred Foot Bank, Welney, Wisbech,
Cambridgeshire, PE14 9TN.
Tel: Ely (0353) 860711

Books Published by THE BOOK CASTLE

JOURNEYS INTO HERTFORDSHIRE: Anthony Mackay.
Foreword by The Marquess of Salisbury, Hatfield House. Nearly 200 superbly detailed ink drawings depict the towns, buildings and landscape of this still predominantly rural county.

JOURNEYS INTO BEDFORDSHIRE: Anthony Mackay.
Foreword by The Marquess of Tavistock, Woburn Abbey.
A lavish book of over 150 evocative ink drawings.

**COUNTRYSIDE CYCLING IN BEDFORDSHIRE,
BUCKINGHAMSHIRE AND HERTFORDSHIRE**: Mick Payne.
Twenty rides on and off-road for all the family.

**LEAFING THROUGH LITERATURE: Writers' Lives in Hertfordshire
and Bedfordshire**: David Carroll.
Illustrated short biographies of many famous authors and their connections with these counties.

THROUGH VISITORS' EYES: A Bedfordshire Anthology:
edited by Simon Houfe.
Impressions of the county by famous visitors over the last four centuries, thematically arranged and illustrated with line drawings.

**THE HILL OF THE MARTYR: An Architectural History of
St. Albans Abbey**: Eileen Roberts.
Scholarly and readable chronological narrative history of Hertfordshire and Bedfordshire's famous cathedral. Fully illustrated with photographs and plans.

LOCAL WALKS: South Bedfordshire and North Chilterns:
Vaughan Basham. Twenty-seven thematic circular walks.

LOCAL WALKS: North and Mid-Bedfordshire:
Vaughan Basham. Twenty-five thematic circular walks.

**CHILTERN WALKS: Hertfordshire, Bedfordshire and
North Buckinghamshire**: Nick Moon.
Part of the trilogy of circular walks, in association with the Chiltern Society. Each volume contains thirty circular walks.

CHILTERN WALKS: Buckinghamshire: Nick Moon.

CHILTERN WALKS: Oxfordshire and West Buckinghamshire:
Nick Moon.

**OXFORDSHIRE WALKS: Oxford, the Cotswolds and the
Cherwell Valley**: Nick Moon.
One of two volumes planned to complement Chiltern Walks: Oxfordshire and complete coverage of the county, in association with the Oxford Fieldpaths Society. Thirty circular walks in each.

**OXFORDSHIRE WALKS: Oxford, the Downs and the
Thames Valley**: Nick Moon.

FOLK: Characters and Events in the History of Bedfordshire and Northamptonshire: Vivienne Evans.
Anthology about people of yesteryear – arranged alphabetically by village or town.

LEGACIES: Tales and Legends of Luton and the North Chilterns: Vic Lea. Twenty-five mysteries and stories based on fact, including Luton Town Football Club. Many photographs.

ECHOES: Tales And Legends of Bedfordshire and Hertfordshire: Vic Lea. Thirty, compulsively retold historical incidents.

ECCENTRICS and VILLAINS, HAUNTINGS and HEROES.
Tales from Four Shires: Northants., Beds., Bucks. and Herts.: John Houghton.
True incidents and curious events covering one thousand years.

THE RAILWAY AGE IN BEDFORDSHIRE: Fred Cockman.
Classic, illustrated account of early railway history.

JOHN BUNYAN: HIS LIFE AND TIMES: Vivienne Evans.
Foreword by the Bishop of Bedford. Preface by Terry Waite. Bedfordshire's most famous son set in his seventeenth century context.

SWANS IN MY KITCHEN: The Story of a Swan Sanctuary: Lis Dorer.
Foreword by Dr Philip Burton. Updated edition. Tales of her dedication to the survival of these beautiful birds through her sanctuary near Hemel Hempstead.

WHIPSNADE WILD ANIMAL PARK: 'MY AFRICA': Lucy Pendar.
Foreword by Andrew Forbes. Introduction by Gerald Durrell. Inside story of sixty years of the Park's animals and people – full of anecdotes, photographs and drawings.

FARM OF MY CHILDHOOD, 1925–1947: Mary Roberts.
An almost vanished lifestyle on a remote farm near Flitwick.

DUNSTABLE WITH THE PRIORY, 1100–1550: Vivienne Evans.
Dramatic growth of Henry I's important new town around a major crossroads.

DUNSTABLE DECADE: THE EIGHTIES: – A Collection of Photographs: Pat Lovering.
A souvenir book of nearly 300 pictures of people and events in the 1980s.

DUNSTABLE IN DETAIL: Nigel Benson.
A hundred of the town's buildings and features, plus town trail map.

OLD DUNSTABLE: Bill Twaddle.
A new edition of this collection of early photographs.

BOURNE AND BRED: A Dunstable Boyhood Between the Wars: Colin Bourne. An elegantly written, well-illustrated book capturing the spirit of the town over fifty years ago.

ROYAL HOUGHTON: Pat Lovering.
Illustrated history of Houghton Regis from the earliest times to the present.

BEDFORDSHIRE'S YESTERYEARS Vol. 1: The Family, Childhood and Schooldays: Brenda Fraser-Newstead.
Unusual early 20th century reminiscences, with private photographs.

BEDFORDSHIRE'S YESTERYEARS Vol 2: The Rural Scene: Brenda Fraser-Newstead.
Vivid first-hand accounts of country life two or three generations ago.

THE CHANGING FACE OF LUTON: An Illustrated History: Stephen Bunker, Robin Holgate and Marian Nichols.
Luton's development from earliest times to the present busy industrial town. Illustrated in colour and monochrome. The three authors from Luton Museum are all experts in local history, archaeology, crafts and social history.

THE MEN WHO WORE STRAW HELMETS: Policing Luton, 1840–1974: Tom Madigan.
Meticulously chronicled history; dozens of rare photographs; author served Luton Police for nearly fifty years.

BETWEEN THE HILLS: The Story of Lilley, a Chiltern Village: Roy Pinnock.
A priceless piece of our heritage – the rural beauty remains but the customs and way of life described here have largely disappeared.

EVA'S STORY: Chesham Since the Turn of the Century: Eva Rance.
The ever-changing twentieth-century, especially the early years at her parents' general stores, Tebby's, in the High Street.

THE TALL HITCHIN SERGEANT: A Victorian Crime Novel based on fact: Edgar Newman. Mixes real police officers and authentic background with an exciting storyline.

Specially for Children

VILLA BELOW THE KNOLLS: A Story of Roman Britain: Michael Dundrow. An exciting adventure for young John in Totternhoe and Dunstable two thousand years ago.

ADVENTURE ON THE KNOLLS: A Story of Iron Age Britain: Michael Dundrow. Excitement on Totternhoe Knolls as ten-year-old John finds himself back in those dangerous times, confronting Julius Caesar and his army.

THE RAVENS: One Boy Against the Might of Rome: James Dyer.
On the Barton Hills and in the south-each of England as the men of the great fort of Ravensburgh (near Hexton) confront the invaders.

Further titles are in preparation.
All the above are available via any bookshop, or from the publisher and bookseller
THE BOOK CASTLE
12 Church Street, Dunstable, Bedfordshire, LU5 4RU
Tel: (0582) 605670